Each recipe includes information on:

– the **number of people** the recipes are intended to serve
– the **preparation and cooking time,** this includes work marinating, and cooking or baking times
– the **nutritional value** per portion

The following symbols and abbreviations are used:

■ = fairly simple
■ ■ = somewhat more time-consuming (more complicated)
■ ■ ■ = demanding

kcal = kilocalories (1 kcal=4.184 kJ)
P = protein
F = fat
C = carbohydrate

NB. 1 gram of protein contains about 4 kcal
1 gram of fat contains about 9 kcal
1 gram of carbohydrate contains about 4 kcal

All temperatures are given for a conventional electric oven, with standard heating elements. If you are using a fan-assisted oven, the oven temperatures should be set 50°F lower than those given for conventional ovens. Times and power information for microwave ovens are given individually in all microwave recipes.

VERSATILE VEGETABLES

AUTHORS AND PHOTOGRAPHY

AN INTRODUCTION TO VEGETABLES

– Friedrich W. Ehlert –
– Odette Teubner, Kerstin Mosny –

HEARTY HOME COOKING

– Rotraud Degner –
– Pete Eising –

DISHES FROM AROUND THE WORLD

– Rotraud Degner –
– Ulrich Kerth –

RECIPES FOR SPECIAL OCCASIONS

– Marianne Kaltenbach –
– Rolf Feuz –

WHOLEFOOD RECIPES

– Doris Katharina Hessler –
– Ansgar Pudenz –

QUICK-AND-EASY RECIPES

– Cornelia Adam –
– Michael Brauner –

MICROWAVE RECIPES

– Monika Kellermann –
– Odette Teubner, Kerstin Mosny –

LEAN CUISINE

– Monika Kellermann –
– Anschlag & Goldmann –

Translated by UPS Translations, London
Edited by Josephine Bacon

CLB 4215
Published originally under the title "Das Neue Menu: Gemüse"
by Mosaik Verlag GmbH, Munich
© Mosaik Verlag, Munich
Project co-ordinator: Peter Schmoeckel
Editors: Ulla Jacobs, Cornelia Klaeger, Heidrun Schaaf, Dr Renate Zeltner
Layout: Peter Pleischl, Paul Wollweber
English translation copyright © 1995 by CLB Publishing, Godalming, Surrey, UK

Published in the USA 1995 by JG Press
Distributed by World Publications, Inc.
Printed and bound in Singapore
ISBN 1-57215-069-6

The JG Press imprint is a trademark of JG Press, Inc.
455 Somerset Avenue
North Dighton, MA 02764

VERSATILE VEGETABLES

JG PRESS

Contents

An Introduction to Vegetables

*W*hether as a side-dish, a main course, or an ingredient in soups and stews, vegetables enhance the taste, appearance, and nutritional value of any meal. Although the roots, stems, leaves, and fruit of plants – which is precisely what vegetables are – used to be boiled to a soft pulp, we now know that the best way to cook vegetables is exactly the opposite. Vegetables that have been conservatively cooked – simmered in a minimum of water – so that they are still firm and crunchy, retain more vitamins and minerals, as well as tasting much better than vegetables which have been boiled until mushy. There are innumerable types of vegetable and just as many ways of preparing them – many of which are presented in this book.

AN INTRODUCTION TO VEGETABLES

VEGETABLES

Vegetables are low in calories, as well as being rich in valuable substances. All vegetables contain vitamins A (carotin), C and B2, minerals such as potassium, magnesium, calcium, iron, and phosphorus, and fiber. However, the amount and combination of minerals and vitamins varies from one vegetable to another, and they vary according to the amount of light, heat, and oxygen to which they have been exposed. Vegetables lying in a bowl, exposed to the light and at room temperature, gradually lose their nutritional value. For this reason, vegetables should always be kept cool and in the dark.

TYPES OF VEGETABLE

The almost unimaginable variety of vegetables can be divided into root vegetables, tuberous vegetables, fruit vegetables, leaf vegetables, shoots, stalk vegetables, bulb vegetables, and legumes. Root and tuberous vegetables include potatoes, carrots, radishes, turnips, rutabaga, and Jerusalem artichokes. Zucchini, eggplant, tomatoes, and peppers represent fruit vegetables, while all types of green salads and turnip greens, collards, and spinach are examples of leaf vegetables. Asparagus, celery, kohlrabi, and fennel, as well as other types of vegetables, belong to the group of shoot and stalk vegetables. All types of onion and garlic are combined in the group of bulbous vegetables. Finally, beans, peas, and lentils are legumes. Mushrooms belong to a separate group of plants and are not technically vegetables because fungi, of which mushrooms are a species, are cryptogams or non-flowering plants.

The classification of vegetables according to the time of year when they are harvested is handy when buying vegetables. Spring vegetables are the first vegetables marketed in that year, for example green onions (scallions), early carrots, turnips, asparagus, and spinach. Globe artichokes, various fruit vegetables, beans, peas, and beet greens are harvested in summer and are therefore known as summer vegetables. Cauliflower and turnips are typical fall vegetables. In winter, the vegetables available include kale, chicory, celery root, Brussels sprouts, beets, carrots, and leeks – these are known as winter vegetables. However, many vegetables are available year-round from the main growing states, California, Texas, and Florida.

A – Z OF VEGETABLES

The following pages provide information such as the nutritional value of vegetables, what to remember when preparing individual types of vegetable, plus other useful facts. The vegetables are arranged in alphabetical order. However, it is impossible to cover fully the enormous range of vegetables available, since about 40 to 50 types of vegetable are currently available in more than 1000 varieties. This huge range is constantly on the increase, both as regards what is commercially available, and varieties that are home-grown.

Artichokes (globe artichokes) are a type of thistle. The green, still unripe flowering head is harvested as a vegetable and has long been an expensive delicacy. In France, artichokes were originally eaten only by French noblemen.

Artichokes contain vitamins A and B and are rich in calcium and iron. They are very easy to digest and also stimulate the digestive system and the liver and gall bladder functions.

Two types of globe artichoke are generally available, large, round, green artichokes with a fleshy base, and small, purple ones with pointed leaves. Both are grown mainly in California and the northeastern United States. They are especially popular with Italian-Americans.

Usually only the base and the fleshy part of the leaves are eaten. This is just 20% of the flower head! However, the tender, fresh stalks, when peeled and boiled, make excellent vegetables and are good in salads.

Artichokes should not be cooked in aluminum or iron saucepans, since they will color them grayish-black.

Storage: about 3 days in the vegetable compartment of the refrigerator.

Asparagus is in season from mid-April to late June.

Green asparagus is most commonly available, but white (blanched) and purple-tipped varieties are popular in central Europe, especially Germany and Italy. Large asparagus spears are expensive, but the thinner grades are cheaper.

Asparagus is extremely low in calories (17 kcal per 100 grams) and contains protein, fiber, and various vitamins and minerals. Its characteristic flavor is derived from volatile oils, vanillin, and other chemical compounds. Green asparagus takes its color from the green pigment chlorophyll, and has a higher vitamin content than white asparagus. In contrast to white asparagus, it should not be peeled, though the lower ends may need scraping.

In addition to green and white asparagus, stronger-flavored asparagus types with yellow or purple tips are also available. Good-quality fresh asparagus has straight stems of equal diameter. If the cut surfaces are scratched they should produce sap.

Storage: 2–3 days wrapped in a damp cloth in the vegetable compartment of the refrigerator. But whenever possible, asparagus should be used fresh.

Belgian endive or witloof chicory was discovered accidentally at the end of the 19th century by Belgian farmers, who found that when grown in the dark it develops strong, pale shoots – endive. Today, Belgium is still the main source of endive in Europe. Endive is grown underground or under black polythene so that it stays tender and pale.

Endive has a bittersweet flavor which not everyone appreciates, but it is rich in vitamins and minerals. In addition, it is considered good for diabetics and people suffering from rheumatism. **Radicchio** is the Italian name given to the red variety of chicory or endive.

When buying endive make sure that it is tightly closed and pale.

Storage: about 4–5 days in the vegetable compartment of the refrigerator, wrapped in damp paper. If kept out too long, the leaves turn light green and the bitter taste becomes stronger.

Broccoli is a member of the cabbage family and is an ancestor of cauliflower. The young flower heads are eaten while still in bud and, in contrast to cauliflower, some of the stalks as well. The delicate cabbage flavor is reminiscent of green asparagus. Compared with other types of cabbage, broccoli is easy to digest and therefore suitable as a light food. It contains primarily vitamins A and C, and calcium.

In addition to green broccoli, there are also red, blue, and purple types. Calabrese is a variety with extra-large tender greeny-blue heads, available in summer; sprouting broccoli is a winter vegetable, producing lots of small spears. If broccoli is blanched before the actual cooking process, the taste is enhanced and the color retained.

Broccoli should always be prepared fresh. Signs of freshness are a bright color and tightly closed flowerets.

Storage: about 2 days in the vegetable compartment of the refrigerator.

Brussels sprouts are one of the finest representatives of the cabbage family. They are typical winter vegetables, which were first grown more than 100 years ago near Brussels, Belgium. If Brussels sprouts are to flourish, the fall must be warm and the winter mild. Sprouts are rich in the minerals potassium, magnesium, iron, and phosphorus, as well as vitamins B and C. Frost increases the sugar content of sprouts, which refines the flavor and makes them easier to digest, since the cellulose tissue (cell structure) is loosened.

Good-quality sprouts should be bright green and firm, with no discolored outer leaves. Avoid small, pale ones: these are stale larger ones which have been trimmed by the store to make them look saleable.

The individual sprouts cook to a firm consistency in 15 minutes or less, according to their size. Cutting a cross in the base of the stalk is often recommended, but is not necessary unless some are larger than others, to ensure that they all cook at the same rate.

Storage: firmly closed sprouts, 2–3 days in the vegetable compartment of the refrigerator.

Cabbage, whether plain green, savoy or white, is always available and, like red cabbage, is a variety of brassica.

Cabbage is a valuable foodstuff. In olden times, sailors protected themselves from scurvy, a disease caused by a lack of vitamin C, by eating pickled cabbage (sauerkraut) in addition to the better-known ration of lime or lemon juice.

Cabbage is still a healthy component of our diets since it is rich in vitamins B1, B2, and C, and in important minerals (iron, magnesium, sodium, and phosphorus).

Cabbage is difficult to digest, but can be made more digestible by blanching in hot salted water or by seasoning with caraway seeds. Cabbage heads should be firmly closed.

Spring greens or spring cabbage is a type of cabbage with a conical head. The large green leaves form a loose cone. It has a more delicate structure and flavor than other types, as well as a shorter storage life. Spring greens are small heads of a leafy green cabbage with no heart.

Storage: up to a fortnight in the vegetable compartment of the refrigerator. Always cover cut surfaces with plastic wrap. Spring cabbage – a maximum of 2 days.

LEGUMES, FRESH AND DRIED

The mature seeds of members of the pea and bean family – legumes – are one of the oldest foodstuffs known. This group includes beans, peas, lentils, and soy beans. Legumes or pulses contain plenty of fiber, bio-logically valuable protein, carbohydrates, minerals, and B-vitamins. Combined with cereals (as in beans on toast), pulses provide a valuable meat substitute.

Fresh peas and beans make the tastiest side-dishes, after only a few minutes' cooking.

Beans come in a wide range of colors and sizes, particularly the dried kinds, but quite a few are also available canned. Popular ones include reddish - flecked pinto beans (12, 7), red kidney beans (15), reddish-black scarlet runner beans (13), olive green mung beans (17) and reddish-brown aduki beans (14). Both the latter types are suitable for germinating and eating as sprouts. In addition there are black beans, green beans, black-eyed peas, great northern beans, lima beans, field beans, the delicate pale green flageolets, and the most valuable bean of all – the soya bean (16).

Most dried beans and peas require soaking to soften them and reduce the cooking time. Broadly speaking, the larger the bean the longer the soaking time; the exceptions are chickpeas (garbanzo beans) and soy beans, which are extremely tough. Lentils do not need soaking. Overnight soaking is often convenient for large or tough beans, but for smaller ones a few hours will suffice, especially if you use boiling water.

Boil the beans in fresh water, quite vigorously at first, then more gently. Do not add salt as this toughens the skins. Cook for as long as needed to make them really tender. Under-cooked or improperly cooked beans can be harmful.

Green or snap beans (8) are among the most widely used. Young, tender beans are suitable for use in salads, while the medium-sized ones are used as a vegetable.

Runner beans (6) are climbing plants grown up poles or strings, and so also known as pole-beans or string-beans. They are usually flat-podded, with quite rough skins, but can also be round-podded. When young they are tender, with good flavor and texture, and can be treated like green beans. But they are sometimes sold far too big, when they are coarse and stringy. Such beans must be de-stringed and finely sliced to be edible. Runner beans are mainly used as a vegetable and in soups.

Wax beans (9) or yellow beans are the yellow variety of the snap bean. They are very tender and best suited for salads.

Baby green beans (10) are very tender, early beans, with a delicate flavor and fine texture. They are divided into three grades – extra, very fine, and fine.

Fava beans are not really beans, but are eaten as such. When dried, the beans are light to dark brown (11).

Unless they are very young, fava beans should not be eaten raw. In this state, they contain the poisonous substance phasin, which can lead to inflammation and stomach complaints. During cooking this heat-sensitive substance is destroyed. So cooking them requires careful timing to ensure that they are tender but still crisp.

Fresh beans are juicy and evenly green or yellow in color. They make a sharp cracking sound when broken in the fingers, which is why they are also known as snap beans.

Storage: about 3 days in the vegetable compartment of the refrigerator, in a plastic bag.

Peas are not only delicious in stews and soups, but can also be made into tasty purées. Yellow (3) and green peas (4, 5) and chickpeas (garbanzo beans) (2) are the best-known types. Dried peas can be obtained either whole or split. Discoveries in various parts of the world indicate that people ate peas as early as 7000 BC. Until well into the Middle Ages, only peas from mature pods were eaten; they were a basic foodstuff as well as a medicine. Then Italian cooks discovered that peas can also be cooked and eaten when green and unripe. Fresh peas in the pod are unfortunately not frequently found in stores, since most are processed for canning or freezing.

Peas are classified according to type and pea size:

Wrinkled peas are sweet and tender, contain mainly carbo-hydrate as sugar, and are almost square.

Round-seeded peas are also known as garden or shelled peas, and are rounded and smooth, with a high starch content, giving them a floury taste.

Snow peas or sugar snap peas (1) are a special variety of pea, eaten whole when the seeds inside have scarcely developed and the pod is paper-thin and extremely tender. Snow peas have almost completely flat pods, while the sugar snaps are more rounded. They are increasingly popular, and are very quick to cook.

Peas in the pod are not tough, and although time-consuming to prepare, are well worth the effort, for the flavor of truly fresh peas is unsurpassed. They can be eaten hot or cold.

The high protein, carbo-hydrate, vitamin, and mineral content of peas makes them a nutritious food. Small, fresh, crisp peas are always the best. The same applies to snow peas. Dried peas, by contrast, should be large.

Storage: 1–2 days in the vegetable compartment of the refrigerator. The boiling time should be doubled after one day's storage.

Lentils have been grown in Asia for thousands of years and today are grown mainly in India and Turkey. The greenish-brown or Puy lentils (20), black (18) and orange or Egyptian lentils (19) are only available dried, either whole or split. As with all pulses, the size determines the price. The smaller and therefore better-value types are, of course, the most tasty. Red or Egyptian lentils have the best flavor of all, and these are usually sold split. They do not take as long to cook as brown lentils.

Soy beans (16) are extremely high in protein and have far and away the highest fat content of all pulses – 100 grams of soy beans contain 18 grams of fat. The whole beans are always eaten dried; they have little flavor and take a long time to cook. However, they are used in many other ways, especially ground into flour or as animal feed. The United States is the world's largest producer of soy beans. Soy beans are used to make soybean oil, lecithin, soy flour, protein concentrate, soy milk, tofu (bean curd), and soy sauce.

Carrots come in two types – short, rounded ones and long, pointed ones. Carrots are an extremely old variety of vegetable, which have been eaten for at least 5000 to 6000 years in central Europe.

They are one of the most popular and frequently used vegetables and contain the greatest amount of carotin (provitamin A) of all. Carotin is only absorbed by the body in combination with fat. Minerals, vitamins C and E, few calories, and easy digestibility make carrots a much-loved ingredient in our diet. They have a sweetish, nutty flavor, as a result of their high fructose content. Young carrots do not require peeling, only scraping or scrubbing, as preferred.

Spring carrots are smaller varieties which have not overwintered. They are about the length and thickness of a finger and are usually sold in bunches with the leaves. They have a sweet, delicate flavor.

Summer carrots are sold from about June to September. They are larger than early carrots.

Late carrots are suitable for storing. They are available from November through March.

Storage: about 3–4 weeks, ventilated and kept cool in a dark place or in the vegetable compartment of the refrigerator.

Cauliflower is one of the few types of vegetable from which the flower head or inflorescence is eaten. Cauliflower has a delicately pronounced cabbage flavor which is easily lost through over-cooking, and it is best steamed or boiled whole rather than cut into flowerets. Its delicate cell structure and relatively high vitamin C and calcium contents endow the cauliflower with its nutritional value. The Romans and Greeks prized cauliflower, not only for its taste. Various healing powers were also attributed to it.

Cauliflower is available in various types. In addition to the well-known white cauliflower, there are also green (romanesco) and purple types. Firm, closed heads are the mark of freshness of this vegetable.

Storage: 3–5 days in the vegetable compartment of the refrigerator.

Celery root (celeriac) looks like a large, misshapen turnip root but tastes strongly of celery. It is actually a swollen stem that grows above ground. It is particularly popular in central Europe, where it can be found during the winter months. It is used in a similar way to celery, makes a flavorsome addition to soups and stews, and can also be eaten raw in salads. To prepare celery root, which is often very knobbly, cut it into thick slices, then peel each slice. Stack the slices and cut them into strips, then into dice. Celery root makes a very good salt substitute. If lemon juice is added to the water it remains white when boiled.

Storage: about 8 days in the vegetable compartment of the refrigerator.

Celery is available all year round in two basic varieties, white and green. The fleshy stalks are rich in Vitamin C and also contain an extremely large amount of potassium. Fresh celery has crisp stalks and green leaves. Because of its crunchiness celery is very good raw, especially with cheese; when cooked, the flavor intensifies and it is eaten as a vegetable or added to stews and soups.

Storage: 1–2 weeks in the vegetable compartment of the refrigerator, kept in its plastic sleeve.

Swiss Chard (Chard or Silverbeet) is an unusual vegetable, a member of the beet family, grown mainly for the large thick stems or ribs, ending in rather coarse green leaves. The common variety has creamy white stems, but there is also one with red stems, known as ruby or rhubarb chard.

Chard is rich in protein and has a vitamin and mineral content similar to those of spinach. It contains primarily the minerals phosphorus, potassium, calcium, magnesium, iron, iodine, and vitamins B1, B2, and C. Chard is recognized as a medicinal plant as a result of its laxative properties and its sedative effects.

The stems and leaves are often cooked separately. The chopped or cut stems are steamed, braised, or boiled, and best served on their own as they have a delicate flavor reminiscent of asparagus. The leaves are cooked in the same way as spinach.

Storage: in the vegetable compartment of the refrigerator. In a plastic bag, the leaves keep for 2–3 days. Wrapped in damp paper, the stems keep for about 8 days.

Corn is not a vegetable, but a cereal grain (maize), which is native to America. The tender, pale golden niblets of sweetcorn are used as a vegetable. Corn contains valuable protein, little fat, and a lot of carbohydrate, in the form of starch. In addition, it also contains vitamins from the B group (particularly niacin) and potassium.

Sweetcorn is the term used to refer to corn off the cob, almost always canned or frozen. It is one of America's favorite vegetables and is also increasing in popularity in Europe.

Corn cobs are harvested when unripe, as soon as the niblets have developed and are juicy. The cob is broken from the stem during harvesting and sold in its leafy shell. Look for cobs with pale gold niblets – if they are dark, the corn was too old when picked and it will be tough. Baby sweetcorn, harvested when immature, is a popular ingredient in Oriental cooking, but has little flavor.

Corn cobs should be boiled for 5–8 minutes in slightly sweetened water, without salt, which stops them from hardening, or broiled or grilled.

Storage: fresh corn keeps for a few days in the vegetable compartment of the refrigerator but is best eaten as soon as possible after picking or purchase.

Cucumber is one of the oldest cultivated plants. It is said to have been grown in India in 4000 BC. In the Middle Ages it became known in Europe. It is a member of the squash family. Long, thin salad cucumbers and fatter, cylindrical ridge cucumbers are suitable in salads and as a vegetable. After sorting according to size, immature, smaller pickling cucumbers are industrially processed into pickles. The smallest are known as cornichons. Both outdoor and green-house cucumbers are available on the market. Cucumbers grown outdoors have a stronger flavor. Cucumbers are extremely low in calories as they consist almost entirely of water, and are rich in vitamins and minerals. Look for cucumbers that are firm, especially at the stalk end. Do not peel unless it is essential to the recipe, as most of the food value lies in the skin.

Storage: 6–7 days in the vegetable compartment of the refrigerator.

Eggplant belongs to the same family as tomatoes, peppers, and potatoes. Originally these vegetables were white or yellow and about the size of a hen's egg, hence the name eggplant or garden egg.

There are two main types available, large, rounded dark purple eggplants, and smaller, narrower, paler varieties, sometimes called Japanese eggplant. The flesh of eggplants contains calcium, iron, and vitamins B and C. Eggplants stimulate the liver and gall bladder functions and have a beneficial effect on rheumatism.

The flavor of these vegetables is only brought out by boiling, roasting, or broiling. Eaten raw, they can cause diarrhea, vomiting, and stomach pains. There is no need to peel eggplants, especially as the dark color of the skin is part of their attraction. Eggplant recipes often include instructions for "degorging" them to remove bitterness, but this is not normally necessary nowadays as eggplants should be nice and fresh when bought. However, if you are particularly sensitive to bitter flavors, simply sprinkle the cut surfaces with salt and leave to drain for about 30 minutes. Salting draws the bitterness out of the fruit, but it also happens to remove the water-soluble vitamins and minerals.

Storage: about 5–6 days in the refrigerator.

Fennel should really be called bulb fennel, to distinguish it from the feathery green tops. While fennel bulbs have been valued for a long time in southern Europe, particularly in Italy, both as a cooked vegetable and in salads, they have been slow to catch on over here. They have a distinct taste of aniseed and go particularly well with fish. There are two types of bulb fennel – Florence fennel, which has a narrow, elongated bulb and a delicate flavor, and Italian fennel, which has a firm, thick bulb and a more pronounced flavor. Fennel contains essential oils which are responsible for its typical flavor, as well as minerals and vitamins C and E. Once sliced, fennel should be sprinkled immediately with lemon juice to maintain its whiteness. It can be eaten raw or cooked and goes well with tomatoes, zucchini, and eggplant.

Storage: at least 14 days in the vegetable compartment of the refrigerator.

Kale is a member of the cabbage family with loose curly green leaves, which was enjoyed as a vegetable in the winter months even before Roman times. It actually comes from the countries around the Mediterranean Sea. Kale is very hardy and only develops its full flavor after the first frosts. For this reason, freezing actually improves the quality of this vegetable, both in terms of taste and nutritional value. Frost breaks down its starch content into sugar, which makes it easier to digest. It contains a great deal of calcium, vitamin A (carotin) and vitamin C. A kilogram (2¼ pounds) of freshly cut kale contains one gram of vitamin C – a vitamin content surpassed only by Brussels sprouts. Kale matches spinach in terms of its mineral content. Fresh kale can be recognized by its stiff green leaves.

Kale can be made into an especially hearty dish if braised with loin of pork, pork sausage, and ham hocks.

Storage: 2–3 days in the vegetable compartment of the refrigerator.

Kohlrabi is probably descended from the type of cabbage eaten in Pompeii by the Romans and was first grown in Europe in the 16th century. It is sometimes called turnip-cabbage but differs from other types in that the round root is eaten and the leaves are usually cut away. Kohlrabi comes in various shapes and colors – rounded or flattened, from almost white, through greenish-white to purple. The color reveals the origin of the kohlrabi. The white variety is usually grown in glasshouses, while the red is grown outdoors. Both varieties have white flesh. Glasshouse kohlrabi has a more delicate structure and taste, while outdoor kohlrabi has a stronger flavor.

Kohlrabi is rich in vitamin C and minerals such as calcium, potassium, phosphorus, magnesium, iron, and sodium.

Young kohlrabi are particularly suitable for vegetable dishes and salads. The leaves, if present, contain a great deal of carotin (vitamin A) and should be used chopped in vegetable dishes and salads.

Storage: 2 days if kept cool and moist. Kohlrabi becomes woody if stored longer than this.

Leeks belong to the extensive onion family and are used as vegetables, for flavoring, and in soups and salads. They are extremely rich in valuable substances, particularly iron, carotin (vitamin A), and vitamins B1, B2, C, and E. They contain the appetite-stimulating sulfurous leek oil, which is responsible for the typical leek smell.

Leeks can be divided into three groups:

Early leeks are tender and mild, with pale green foliage and a white stalk. They are highly suitable for use as vegetables, in soups, and as a flavoring. They are also suitable for eating raw with mixed raw vegetables and in salads.

Summer leeks have thin skins and a long white, fairly strong stalk, with green foliage. They are delicious eaten as a cooked vegetable.

Winter leeks have greenish-blue foliage and a strong, short stalk. The foliage has a strong flavor, while the stalk is mild and delicate. In winter, blanched leeks are also available. Their white color is caused by the lack of light. The soil is heaped up around the stalks, which also makes them hard.

Storage: 10–12 days in the vegetable compartment of the refrigerator.

Onions are indispensable in cooking, both as a flavoring and a vegetable. In addition to vitamins A and C, they also contain minerals such as potassium and magnesium, and they have an antibacterial effect.

The following types of onion are available in the stores:

The brown onion, which has the strongest flavor, is the most common; the color of the flesh ranges from white to yellow.

The Bermuda onion is the largest and mildest. Its flesh is juicy and is suitable for eating raw in salads or with bread and cheese, roasting, baking, stuffing, and boiling.

The green onion or scallion is a miniature variety picked when the bulbs are barely developed. It is eaten raw in salads and is an important component of Chinese cooking. The green tops are a good substitute for chives.

The red or salad onion has a spicy but mild flavor compared with the common brown onion. It is good in salads, and can be used in cooked dishes.

Shallots, the smallest and finest representatives of the onion family, are very popular in French cuisine. They have a very delicate flavor and are used in classic sauces, regional dishes, and salads.

Storage: several weeks if kept cool and dry.

Peas: see Legumes

Peppers should actually be referred to as sweet peppers, bell peppers, or capsicums to distinguish them from their much hotter relative, the chili pepper. The most commonly available are bell-shaped and green, red, yellow, or purple. In addition to carbohydrate and protein, they contain important minerals and vitamins, including ten times more vitamin C than lemons. The white cores and membranes contain capsaicin, which gives peppers their spicy flavor.

Hot peppers or chilies are also members of the capsicum family, but are much smaller. They originate from central America, where endless different varieties are used, with varying degrees of hotness. Green chilies are generally hotter than red (ripe) ones. They are used whenever a hot taste is required in a dish, notably in chili con carne, and to make cayenne pepper and paprika. When preparing chilies, wash your hands and equipment thoroughly afterward, and be very careful not to get the juice in your eyes via your fingers since it is a powerful irritant. If fresh chilies are not available, dried ones are a good substitute.
Storage: 3–5 days in the vegetable compartment of the refrigerator.

Red cabbage is a type of head cabbage and has been enjoyed as a vegetable since the 8th century. It differs from other head cabbages in that it has a higher vitamin C content. In addition, it is easier to digest, contains more fiber, and is purplish-red in color. The leaves turn a deeper red with the addition of acid, which is why most recipes for cooking it include a little vinegar, wine, lemon juice, or tart apple. It goes especially well with pork and game. Red cabbage should never be boiled in an aluminum saucepan, because the red dye reacts with aluminum and loses its strength and the cabbage turns a bluish color. Red cabbage is available almost all year round, as early cabbage, semi-early cabbage, and fall cabbage.
Storage: up to 14 days in the vegetable compartment of the refrigerator. Always cover a cut cabbage with foil.

Salsify (scorzonera, black salsify or oyster plant) is relatively uncommon in the US, although popular in Europe. It is a winter root vegetable which has been cultivated since the 17th century. Its wild form, which is native to southern Europe, has been used as a medicinal plant. Salsify is highly nutritious, mainly as a result of its carbohydrate, mineral (potassium, calcium, phosphorus, and iron) and vitamin contents. Its inulin content is particularly noteworthy. This is a carbohydrate made from fructose. When peeled, salsify produces a milky juice that stains the skin, so it should be handled with rubber gloves. It also discolors rapidly after peeling, but this can be prevented by immediately putting each root into water with a little vinegar added. When buying salsify, make sure the surface is smooth and the flesh pale and juicy.
Storage: 14 days in the vegetable compartment of the refrigerator, wrapped in paper.

Savoy cabbage is another popular type of cabbage, in addition to the green and red varieties. It comes from the northern Mediterranean area and was cooked as long ago as the Middle Ages.
Savoy cabbage is not as tightly closed as red and green cabbage types. Its leaves are wrinkled and curly. It comes in many colors, from dark green to yellow. The dark green early Savoy cabbage is the most valued variety. In addition to the early variety, Savoy cabbage is also available in fall and winter varieties. Savoy cabbage keeps the least well of all cabbage types. It is cooked in the same way as the other types and goes well with game and lamb.
Dark green Savoy cabbage contains more valuable nutrients than white cabbage and is also easier to digest.
Storage: about 14 days in the vegetable compartment of the refrigerator.

Spinach has a relatively high iron content in comparison with other vegetables. Many vegetables contain between 1 and 3 milligrams of iron per 100 grams, but spinach contains over 4 milligrams per 100 grams.

By contrast, it should be noted that spinach is high in nitrates, which are further increased by the use of chemical fertilizers. Oxygen (air) and heat convert nitrates into poisonous nitrites, which are particularly harmful to children. For this reason, spinach should only be used fresh (without being stored) and should not be reheated. The nitrate level can also be reduced by thorough washing. Cook while still wet without adding any extra water; cover the pan and shake it from time to time. Spinach shrinks greatly during cooking, so buy at least 8 ounces per person. Fresh spinach should be crisp and dark green.

Beet and turnip greens look very similar to spinach and are sometimes sold as such. The leaves are larger and the stems coarser; remove these when washing. Otherwise treat these leaves exactly like spinach.

Storage: not recommended.

Tomatoes were first grown in Italy and in the southeastern Mediterranean area. Tomatoes are rich in minerals and vitamins, especially vitamin C. Round tomatoes account for the largest market share. They are suitable for both cooking and salads Their sweet-and-sour flavor can be enhanced by adding a pinch of sugar. Green parts, which should always be removed before eating, indicate the presence of the toxic substance solanin.

Beefsteak tomatoes are large, with a very fruity flavor and a high proportion of flesh. They are best enjoyed raw but can also be used in hot dishes.

Plum tomatoes are named for their shape, and are the ones which are usually sold canned. They have an excellent flavor but this only develops with cooking, so they are not at their best in salads, although very firm and with a deep red color. The canned ones are excellent for use in stews.

Cherry tomatoes are a relative novelty. These miniature tomatoes have a fruity flavor and are ideal for garnishing and salads.

Storage: several days at room temperature, longer in the refrigerator.

Turnips come in various shapes and sizes and used to be extremely popular in Europe, but have now been displaced by the potato. During periods of crisis and in wartime they have always experienced an upswing in consumption. Most turnips do not contain any important nutrients, but all types are low in calories and are excellent for flavoring soups and stews.

Baby or white turnips are the first of the year, with a white skin, white flesh, and a sweetish flavor. They taste best when they are about the size of a hen's egg, and do not need peeling.

French turnips are a small variety, rather flattened, with pale, purple-and-white skins which should not be peeled. The flavor is delicate, rather like that of kohlrabi.

Late turnips are larger than baby turnips, with white flesh and a sharp flavor. They are good with lamb and pork.

Rutabaga are larger than turnips, greenish-yellow or purplish-yellow on the outside, and with pale orange flesh on the inside. They are a good winter vegetable, suitable for use in stews and soups. They are also delicious cooked and mashed with plenty of butter and pepper.

Storage: about 1 week in the vegetable compartment of the refrigerator.

Zucchini belong to the gourd or squash family. They are native to America where they have been grown for over 6000 years. Zucchini, together with avocados and chilies, are among the oldest cultivated plants.

"Zucchino" is the diminutive form of the Italian word "zucca", meaning gourd. Zucchini are harvested when unripe and only 6–8 in long; at this stage they have no seeds in the center. They are usually dark green but there are also types which are flecked or striped white, entirely white, yellow, and golden. Young, tender zucchini do not have to be peeled, but some people find the skin of larger ones slightly bitter. They are boiled or fried in vegetable dishes, and can also be added raw to salads. The flowers, known as squash blossoms, used in native American cooking, are enjoying increasing popularity in our kitchens.

Like all squashes, zucchini contain a great deal of water, are low in calories, and rich in vitamins.

Storage: 3–4 days in the vegetable compartment of the refrigerator or other cool place.

POTATOES

Potatoes are one of our major basic foodstuffs. They originated in the central highlands and coastal area of the Andes. In the 16th century, sailors brought this nondescript tuber to Europe, via Virginia where they were first grown in what is now the United States. Today, nutritious and vitamin-rich potatoes are indispensable in our cuisine. The starchy tubers contain a relatively large amount of calcium, iron, potassium, sodium, and phosphorous, vitamins A, B1, B2, and C. Green potatoes contain the toxin solanin and for this reason should not be eaten.

The range of possibilities for using potatoes is enormous. Whether boiled or steamed, roasted or baked, fried or sautéed, made into hash browns, home fries, French fries, gratins, soups or stews, they always taste good!

TYPES

There are currently between 100 and 120 types of potato, only a few of which are marketed. They are subdivided as follows:

Earlies: available October through February. Usually sold as new potatoes for immediate use.

Maincrop: available from fall. Suitable for storing in a frost-free dark place, but do not refrigerate for long storage.

TEXTURE

Potatoes are not only classified according to type, but also according to their texture once cooked, which is determined by their starch content. The earlier the potatoes ripen, the less starch they contain, and the firmer they are when cooked. Only the older types accumulate so much starch during the summer that they become light and floury when cooked. All the available types of potato fall into one of three cooking categories (see table). Buy from good stores and markets where the varieties are properly labeled, so that you can be sure they will be suitable for your purpose.

Waxy potatoes have a low starch content and do not fall apart when cooked. They are firm and should be used for potato salads, unpeeled boiled potatoes, and plain boiled potatoes. Examples are Long Whites such as White Rose and Round Reds such as Red LaSola and Red Pontiac.

All-purpose potatoes have an average starch content. They remain firm when cooked and are slightly floury. During boiling, the skins split open. Some are mainly waxy and suitable for potato salads and for unpeeled boiled potatoes, but most are good all-rounders, used for roasting, boiling, French fries, and baking. Examples are Round Whites such as Katahdin (grown predominantly in Maine) and the ubiquitous Russet Burbank, the Idaho potato.

Floury potatoes have a high starch content. After cooking, they are floury, dry, and light. They also tend to be large, and are ideal for mashing and baking. Russet Burbank is the best example.

After a long absence of "interesting" varieties, some delicious and attractive potatoes, such as the yellow Finnish Yellow Wax and the Blue Carib and All Blue, with their grayish-blue skins and dark blue flesh are starting to appear. Look out for them at farmers' markets. They will certainly be the highlight of a festive dinner!

STORAGE

Smaller quantities of potatoes should be kept cool, if possible in the dark and ventilated (preferably in a cardboard box). Carefully remove all plastic packaging. If storing larger quantities for a longer period, or putting them in a cellar or outhouse, bear in mind the following:-

Potatoes for storing must be fully ripe with a firm, undamaged skin; if possible they should be clean. On no account should potatoes be washed before storing. A thin layer of dry soil on the skin does no harm and even provides protection against rotting. The ideal storage temperature is around 40°F. Cool, dry, dark cellars or storerooms make good storage places, but they must always be frost-free and well ventilated. Frost eventually converts the starch into sugar and gives the potatoes a slightly sweet taste. Adequate ventilation, particularly from below, is important. Paper sacks or plastic mesh bags are suitable, but they should not be piled higher than 16 inches. Never store in plastic bags. If the potatoes are not in paper sacks it is worth loosely covering them with newspaper, since light can cause green patches to form, and these contain toxic solanin (any green patches should be cut out before cooking). Sprouting potatoes should be used quickly; remove the sprouts before cooking.

SUMMARY OF COOKING TYPE AND STORAGE LIFE OF SOME POPULAR TYPES OF POTATO

Types	Cooking characteristics	Storage
earlies (scrapers)		
Round Reds	soft waxy texture	intended for immediate
Round Whites	soft waxy texture	use after harversting
Finnish Yellow Wax	firm waxy texture	use after harversting
maincrop		
Round Whites	firm texture	suitable for long storage
Russet Burbank	floury texture	suitable for long storage
Long Whites	firm texture	suitable for long storage

MUSHROOMS

Mushrooms are used as vegetables, but they are fungi which belong to a separate, large botanical group.

In terms of nutritional value, edible mushrooms are similar to vegetables. In terms of minerals, they contain primarily potassium and phosphorus. They also contain vitamin D, which occurs very rarely in green vegetables. Since the cell walls of mushrooms contain chitin and cellulose, they are difficult to digest. Even mushroom protein is relatively difficult to digest and is poorly absorbed by the body.

Ordinary closed cup or button so-called store (cultivated) mushrooms are often the only types available. But other types are slowly coming onto the market, and the following are the most likely to be found:

Birch boletus (4) are closely related to the cep and are associated mainly with birch trees. They have white flesh which quickly discolors and yellow pores. As soon as the cap and stalk have been cut, it becomes deep red to violet in color. These wild fungi have an aromatic flavor and go well with game dishes.

Boletus luteus (8) is a close relative of the cep. It has white, butter-soft flesh. The slimy brown skin of the cap can easily be removed.

Storage: this mushroom deteriorates quickly and should be used immediately.

Ceps or Porcini (10) grow in deciduous and coniferous forests. The cap of young mushrooms is light brown and hemi-spherical. Older ones have red to dark brown, parasol-like caps. Thanks to their nutty flavor, ceps have a wide variety of uses; they are widely used in the production of canned and packaged soups. They are also suitable for use raw in salads.

Storage: use immediately. Dried mushrooms should be soaked in cold water for a little while before use.

Chanterelles (9). These bright yellow edible mushrooms with funnel-shaped caps grow in deciduous and coniferous forests. They can be prepared almost without waste and are suitable as an accompaniment to game dishes, egg dishes, or as a flavoring for sauces.

Storage: fresh mushrooms can be kept for one or two days in the vegetable compartment of the refrigerator or in a cool, dark place. Chanterelles become very tough if allowed to dry out and are less suitable for deep-frying, since this gives them a bitter taste.

Cultivated or store (1, 3) or brown mushrooms (2) are the best known and most widely used edible mushrooms. They are always available. The caps of young mushrooms are still firmly closed and have grown with the stalk. The cap gradually opens as the mushroom ages and the color of the pink gills changes to dark brown, via dark pink. The progressive stages are known as button, closed cup, open cup, and flat.

Fresh button or closed cup mushrooms should be firm and crisp. If the stalk ends are dark, this indicates that the mushrooms have been stored for some time. Button mushrooms are ideal for cooking whole, or for use in creamy sauces, as the pale gills cause no discoloration. Closed cup mushrooms are extremely versatile and can be fried, braised, stewed, or broiled; they are especially tasty raw in salads. Open cup mushrooms are good for frying, stuffing, and baking; flat mushrooms are only suitable for use in stews and mushroom soup as they impart a dark color, but they have the best flavor. Brown mushrooms, sometimes labeled chestnut mushrooms, have a stronger flavor than the white types, but are not so widely available.

These mushrooms are grown in sterile conditions and do not need peeling or washing, just wiping with absorbent paper.

Storage: mushrooms pre-packaged in plastic wrap should be removed from the packaging after purchase. If the mushrooms are fresh, firm, and not too damp, they will stay fresh in the vegetable compartment of the refrigerator for a few days. Closed cup mushrooms which have dried during storage can still be used if soaked in milk for a little while before cooking.

Morels (6) are some of the most strongly-flavored edible mushrooms of the genus Morchella. The stalk is wrinkled and hollow, the cap is pitted and honeycomb-like. Depending on the shape of the cap, a distinction is made between round and pointed morels. Since fresh morels are very sandy, they must be thoroughly washed before use. Dried morels need to be soaked for 2 hours, after which they still have to be washed. Morels make an excellent substitute for truffles, but must never be eaten raw.

Storage: eat fresh ones as soon as possible. These mushrooms should not be stored.

Oyster mushrooms (5) or oyster fungus. The cap ranges from ¼ inch to 6 inches across, is rounded or semi-circular, and varies in color from gray/mauve and bluish-gray to olive/black. There are also yellow to brownish types. Oyster mushrooms are mildly aromatic with a delicate flavor. When bought they should feel firm; small to medium ones are preferable to larger ones. In addition to their many uses as a side - dish or flavoring, the caps can also be breaded and fried like steaks. They are often used in oriental cuisine.

Storage: if not used immediately, they are best stored in the refrigerator, preferably in the vegetable compartment, or in a cool, dark place for a further 2 to 3 days. Dried ones should be soaked briefly in hot water.

Shiitake mushrooms (7) came originally from Japan, where they have been cultivated for many centuries. They have been commercially available for only a short time but are gaining in popularity due to their strong spicy flavor and pronounced aroma. The mushrooms have a slightly ribbed, pale to dark brown cap, covered in pale scales. If it is fresh, the cap should be cup-shaped. Shiitake mushrooms are mainly suitable for Oriental cuisine, particularly stews.

Storage: they will stay fresh for a few days if stored loosely in a cool, dark place.

Truffles (11, 12) are bulbous fungi, covered in a rough skin. They have firm flesh. Specially trained dogs or pigs are sometimes used to find these fungi, which grow underground mainly in Europe, though one variety has been found in Texas. The best black truffles come from southern France (Périgord truffles). White truffles come from northern Italy (Piedmont truffles) and are usually sliced wafer-thin, and scattered raw over food. All truffles are expensive imported luxuries, available only from gourmet food stores.

TIPS FOR BUYING VEGETABLES

Healthy eating means buying vegetables which are in season at a given time of year, because artificial after-ripening and long transportation reduce the levels of valuable nutrients. In addition, glasshouse vegetables contain a higher level of harmful chemicals (fertilizer residues and nitrates) than vegetables grown outdoors.

Organically-grown vegetables may not be entirely free of harmful substances, but they do contain considerably fewer than conventionally cultivated vegetables.

Although most vegetables are available all year round, some vegetables are most definitely seasonal. Since vegetable growing is dependent upon the weather, changes in the times shown on the vegetable calendar cannot be ruled out. When fresh vegetables are not available, frozen vegetables are recommended as an alternative. Vegetables are more efficiently frozen in bulk than in a home freezer.

STORING VEGETABLES CORRECTLY

It goes without saying that vegetables should always be eaten when they are as fresh as possible, but often stocking up on vegetables cannot be avoided. Almost all vegetables can be stored in the vegetable compartment of the refrigerator, loosely packed and at the correct temperature. However, each vegetable type has its own individual storage time (see THE A–Z OF VEGETABLES). Vegetables can be stored for several months in the freezer compartment or in a chest freezer. It is important only to freeze fresh, undamaged, blanched vegetables. Some types of vegetable should be cooked before freezing, for example eggplant, endive, and some types of bean.

Storage times vary from 3 months (eggplant) to 10 months (types of cabbage, legumes).

Industrially frozen vegetables provide another storage possibility, where small portions can be sold. Prepared frozen vegetables can be stored for several weeks in a home freezer compartment or chest freezer. When buying these products, make sure that the packaging is not damaged. The time which elapses between buying them and putting them back into storage should be short, so that the vegetables do not thaw. Thawed or defrosted vegetables must be used immediately.

Yet another way of storing vegetables is to bottle or pickle them in liquid made from vinegar, salt, sugar, and spices. Vinegar prevents the development of mold and putrifying or fermenting bacteria. The correct mixture of vinegar and other ingredients gives vegetables a spicy, sweet-and-sour flavor. Pickled vegetables go well with meat dishes.

TRIMMING, WASHING, AND CHOPPING VEGETABLES

Before cooking, vegetables have to be trimmed, washed, and sliced or diced. Whether to peel them or not is largely a matter of personal taste, but in the interests of healthy eating one should remember that a lot of vitamins and minerals are concentrated in the skin. Onions and garlic are always peeled. Trimmed vegetables should never be washed after chopping or slicing, to prevent water-soluble vitamins and minerals from leaching out. If chopped vegetables are not to be used immediately, they should be covered with a damp cloth. This protects the vegetables from reacting with oxygen (oxidation), which often turns vegetables brown. Sprinkling vegetables with lemon juice or vinegar also prevents this discoloration.

VEGETABLE CALENDAR

The months shown on the calendar indicate the main harvesting period in the northern United States. Almost all types are available outside these months as imports from Florida, California, Arizona, and Texas.

Vegetable	J	F	M	A	M	J	J	A	S	O	N	D
Artichoke				■	■	■						
Asparagus				■	■	■						
Broccoli					■	■	■	■	■	■	■	■
Brussels sprouts	■	■								■	■	■
Carrots	■	■	■	■	■	■	■	■	■	■	■	■
Cauliflower						■	■	■	■	■	■	■
Celeriac (celery root)	■	■	■						■	■	■	■
Celery								■	■	■	■	■
Chicory and endive	■	■	■						■	■	■	■
Green cabbage									■	■	■	■
Corn							■	■	■	■		
Cucumber						■	■	■	■	■		
Eggplant						■	■	■	■	■		
Fennel						■	■	■	■	■	■	■
Green beans						■	■	■	■	■		
Kohlrabi					■	■	■	■	■	■		
Leeks							■	■	■	■	■	■
Onions							■	■	■	■	■	■
Peas				■	■	■	■	■				
Peppers and chilis							■	■	■	■		
Red cabbage	■	■	■	■	■	■	■	■	■	■	■	■
Savoy cabbage	■	■	■	■	■					■	■	■
Salsify (Oyster plant)	■								■	■	■	■
Spinach			■	■	■	■			■	■	■	
Swiss Chard (silverbeet)							■	■	■	■		
Tomatoes						■	■	■	■	■		
Turnips and rutabaga	■	■				■	■	■	■	■	■	■
White cabbage	■	■	■					■	■	■	■	■
Zucchini							■	■	■	■		

COOKING VEGETABLES

Regardless of how vegetables are cooked, the process should be quick so that the vegetables stay firm and lose as few vitamins in the water as possible.

It is not necessary to arrange the following cooking methods by type of vegetable, since almost all vegetables can be cooked in any of these ways. Green beans, for example, can be blanched, boiled, steamed, or braised.

Blanching means boiling vegetables briefly in water and then cooling them in cold water. To prevent the vitamins leaching out excessively, a little salt should be added to the water. If vinegar or lemon juice is added to the water the vegetables will retain more color.

Blanching makes vegetables tastier and easier to work with, particularly spinach and some types of cabbage. It takes the bitterness out of endive, prepares vegetables for freezing, makes the skin easier to remove (tomatoes, for example) and makes leaf vegetables easier to shape.

Blanching times vary between a few seconds for delicate vegetables (young spinach, tomatoes) and 2–4 minutes for more sturdy types (cabbage.) Except for spinach, the blanching water should be saved because it contains many nutrients and can be used in sauces and soups.

Steaming without pressure is a fat-free, extremely gentle cooking method, which involves cooking the vegetables in water vapor. The vegetables do not come into contact with water. All you need is a saucepan with

Fresh vegetables in great variety are available all year round.

a tight-fitting lid and a steamer. Fill the saucepan with about 1½ inches of water. Season and bring to the boil. Then place the vegetables in the steamer over the saucepan and steam gently, depending on type. Using this method, many vegetables take between 15 and 20 minutes to cook.

Steaming under pressure has its advantages and disadvantages. Although the shorter cooking time does retain the nutrients better, the flavors cannot develop properly during this time. The vegetables therefore have less flavor than when cooked without pressure. A pressure-cooker should only be used when time is genuinely of the essence. The cooking times given in recipes must be observed carefully to prevent over-cooking the vegetables.

Sweating is another gentle way of cooking vegetables. This involves cooking chopped or sliced vegetables with a little fat and/or liquid, at just below boiling point. Use a large skillet so that the vegetables can lie flat next to each other. First heat the fat, then add the vegetables and seasoning, including salt, cover, and sweat for 1–2 minutes. This allows the

typical aromas and flavors of the vegetables to develop. Only then should a little water be added and the vegetables cooked over a low heat until firm. When the cooking process is complete only a little liquid should be left. Cooking times may be a little longer than for steaming without pressure.

Glazing is a version of sweating. As well as fat and/or liquid, sugar is also added to the saucepan, so that the vegetables are given a shiny coating. It is important to remove the lid when two-thirds of the cooking time has elapsed so that most of the liquid can evaporate. In addition, the vegetables should be tossed frequently during cooking. Pearl onions, turnips, carrots, and chestnuts are especially suitable for cooking in this way.

Boiling means cooking in bubbling, slightly salted liquid in a saucepan with a tight-fitting lid. This cooking method causes the most leaching from vegetables which is why it is best for cooking whole vegetables, such as potatoes, carrots, and peas. There should be sufficient water in the saucepan just to barely cover the vegetables. The veg-

etables should be placed straight into the vigorously boiling water, then cooked until firm in water which is just boiling gently.

Braising is usually only used for stuffed vegetable dishes (such as eggplant, cucumber, zucchini, and cabbage). The stuffed vegetable should be placed on a bed of finely-chopped vegetables, such as carrot slices and onion rings. First, brown all the vegetables and then just cover in liquid (vegetable broth) and cook in the oven. Braising juices from which the fat has been skimmed make a good base for vegetable broth.

Shallow frying (sautéeing) is good for sliced vegetables such as eggplant, zucchini, artichoke hearts, potatoes, and mushrooms. Season the vegetable slices and sauté them in oil or butter. Place on absorbent paper afterward to remove excess fat.

COOKING FROZEN VEGETABLES

Frozen vegetables can be sweated or boiled. To sweat, place a little butter, the frozen vegetables, a little liquid, and seasoning in a saucepan. Cover and sweat. To boil, place the frozen vegetables in vigorously boiling salted water and cook, covered. Cooking times for frozen vegetables are much shorter than for fresh vegetables because they have been blanched before freezing, and because the cell structure of the vegetables loosens with freezing.

COOKING WHOLE ARTICHOKES

1. Always break off the stalk right next to the base so that the fibers in the heart come away with the stalk.

2. Cut about 1½–2 inches from the leaf tips, using a carving knife.

3. Remove the small lower leaves and cut away the remaining leaves from the base using a sharp knife.

4. Remove the tips from the remaining leaves using scissors. If the prepared artichoke is not to be cooked immediately, soak it in slightly salted, acidulated water.

5. Put the artichoke in salted, boiling water to which a few drops of lemon juice have been added, cover, and simmer for 20 minutes.

6. Twist out the inner leaves; set aside.

7. Using a sharp spoon, scoop out the choke from the heart. Replace the inner leaves, upside-down.

3.

4.

5.

COOKING ARTICHOKE HEARTS

1. Pull off the stalk right next to the base so that the fibers come away with the stalk. Remove the outer leaves by hand.

2. Carefully cut off the medium-sized leaves immediately above the base, using a large sharp knife.

3. Now carefully remove any remaining leaves from the base, using a small sharp knife.

4. Using a sharp spoon, remove all of the inedible choke.

5. Either rub the prepared artichoke heart with lemon or place in slightly salted acidulated water before boiling, so that it does not discolor.

6. Boil the hearts in salted water, to which a few drops of lemon juice have been added, until just tender.

3.

4.

5.

6.

1.

2.

6.

7.

1.

2.

6.

Artichoke heart

STUFFING EGGPLANT

1. Halve the eggplants lengthwise. Make several criss-cross incisions in the flesh, using a sharp knife.
2. Place the halves, cut surfaces face downward, on a lightly-oiled baking sheet and brown in the oven.
3. When the eggplant flesh is soft, remove it using a sharp spoon or a melon-baller.
4. Mix the chopped flesh with 1 cup ground raw meat, a finely diced red pepper, 3 tablespoons of cooked rice and 2 crushed garlic cloves. Season with salt, pepper, and cayenne pepper and use the mixture to fill the eggplant halves.
5. Place the stuffed eggplants in a buttered ovenproof dish. Cover with sliced tomato, sprinkle with grated cheese, and drizzle with oil.
6. Bake in the oven until browned.

3.

4.

5.

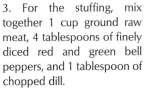

STUFFING CUCUMBERS

1. Thinly peel the cucumbers, removing each end.
2. Cut the cucumbers in half crosswise. Using a thin wooden spoon handle, loosen the core, then carefully push it out using a thicker handle.
3. For the stuffing, mix together 1 cup ground raw meat, 4 tablespoons of finely diced red and green bell peppers, and 1 tablespoon of chopped dill.
4. Put the stuffing into a piping bag fitted with a large nozzle and pipe into the cucumbers.
5. Butter a flat, ovenproof dish and cover it with slices of carrot and onion. Place the cucumbers on top.
6. Season the cucumbers with salt, pepper, and a pinch of sugar. Barely cover with broth and cover the container with a lid or with aluminum foil.
7. Bring to the boil, then cook in a moderate oven for about 25 minutes.

3.

4.

5.

1.

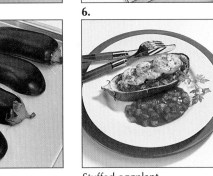

6.

1.

6.

2.

Stuffed eggplant

2.

7.

SLICING ONIONS

1. Cut the onion in half lengthwise, then cut off the root end and the tip.

2. Cut the prepared onion lengthwise into slices.

3. For onion rings, first cut the tip from the whole onion. Then cut the onion crosswise into thin, even slices.

CHOPPING ONIONS

1. Halve the onions lengthwise and make a vertical cut to just above the root.

2. Make several tiny horizontal cuts in each onion half.

3. Finally, hold the onion firmly and slice thinly; it will fall into fine dice.

PREPARING TOMATOES

1. Remove the stalks. Using a small sharp knife, cut a shallow cross in the base of each tomato.

2. Briefly plunge into boiling water or pour boiling water over the tomatoes.

3. Cool immediately in cold water, peel, and at the same time cut out the stem end, which contains solanin, and any green parts.

4. To remove the seeds, halve the tomato and scoop them out with a small sharp spoon, without damaging the outer wall of the fruit.

5. For salads, wash thoroughly, cut out the stalk end by making a cone-shaped incision in the fruit, and cut into thin slices using a very sharp knife.

COOKING ASPARAGUS

1. If using white (blanched) asparagus, peel before cooking. Peel the stalk from tip to base, using a swivel-action vegetable peeler.
2. Wash the asparagus and divide it into bundles. Loosely tie each portion together with kitchen string, so that the tips are all at the same level.
3. Trim the base of the asparagus spears to the same length.
4. Add 1 tablespoon of salt and 1 teaspoon of sugar to 1 quart of water. Cook the asparagus in the water for about 15–18 minutes.

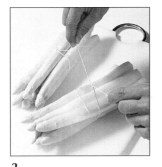

2.

3.

BLANCHING BROCCOLI

1. Remove any leaves from the broccoli. Divide the head into flowerets and wash them under cold running water.
2. Peel any large coarse stalks and cut them into slices.
3. To blanch, put the broccoli flowerets and the stalks into boiling, salted water for 2–3 minutes.
4. Remove the broccoli from the boiling water and cool in cold water (do not add ice cubes).
5. Place the broccoli in a colander to drain.

3.

4.

1.

1.

2.

1.

4.

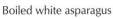

Boiled white asparagus

Broccoli ready to serve

Hearty Home Cooking

This first chapter brings together the best vegetable recipes using the kind of vegetables that used to be available in abundance from every backyard, but giving you new and exciting ways in which to use them. These are the inexpensive vegetables that are so nourishing and sustaining, such as fava beans, cabbage, collard greens, potatoes, and Brussels sprouts. If some of the quantities seem large (as in the fava bean recipe on page 36) or the vegetables hard to find (as with fresh grated horseradish on page 39) this is because we know that people like to grow these traditional crops in their own gardens or yards.

*Beets with Bacon
(see recipe on page 39)*

MUSHROOMS IN CREAM SAUCE

SERVES 4 ■

*Preparation and cooking
time: 30 minutes
Kcal per portion: 450
P = 9g, F = 41g, C = 6g*

*10 cups button mushrooms
2 shallots
½ cup butter
juice of ½ lemon
1 cup light cream
salt and pepper
2 tbsps brandy
1 tbsp chopped chervil*

*Cut off the stalk ends, then wipe
the mushrooms.*

1. Cut off the mushroom
stalks (use these in soup)
and wipe the mushrooms
with absorbent paper. Slice
the mushrooms evenly.
Finely chop the shallots.
2. Heat the butter in a large
skillet and sweat the shallots
until transparent. Add the
mushrooms and continue
cooking until all the liquid
has evaporated and the
mushrooms begin to turn
color. Add the lemon juice.
3. Put the cream in a small
saucepan and bring to the
boil. Add almost all of it to
the mushrooms and cook
over medium heat until
reduced. Season with salt
and pepper to taste.
4. Combine the brandy with
the remaining cream and
pour this over the mush-
rooms. Bring back to the
boil, then remove from the
heat. Serve immediately,
sprinkled with chervil.
Accompaniment: new potatoes; or arrange on four
slices of toast and serve as
an appetizer.

*Braise the thinly sliced
mushrooms in butter with the
diced shallots.*

*Heat most of the cream, pour it
over the vegetables, and reduce.*

FAVA BEANS

SERVES 4 ■

*Preparation and cooking
time: 1 hour
Kcal per portion: 1425
P = 88g, F = 37g, C = 184g*

*5 pounds fresh fava beans in
the pod
6 slices smoked rindless
Canadian bacon
20 green onions (scallions)
(white parts only)
1 large onion
1 bunch parsley
1 tbsp oil
2 cups vegetable broth
1 tsp dried savory
salt and pepper
2 tbsps plain yogurt*

1. Remove the beans from
their pods and wash them.
Finely dice the bacon.
2. Wash and trim the green
onions. Finely chop the
onion and parsley.
3. Melt the oil in a casserole
and sweat the bacon until
the fat is transparent. Add
the onion and parsley
(reserve some parsley for
garnishing), and sweat
briefly. Add the beans and
sauté for a few minutes.
4. Pour the broth over the
vegetables. Add the savory,
salt, and pepper. Cook the
beans over a medium heat
for about 40 minutes.
5. 10 minutes before the end
of the cooking time, remove
the lid so that the liquid can
reduce completely.
6. Add the yogurt to the vegetables and bring to the boil.
Serve sprinkled with the
reserved parsley.
Accompaniment: new potatoes.

KOHLRABI

SERVES 4 ■

*Preparation and cooking
time: 25 minutes
Kcal per portion: 115
P = 4g, F = 6g, C = 10g*

*6 young kohlrabi
1 cup water
salt
2 tbsps softened butter
1 tbsp flour
freshly grated nutmeg*

*First remove any green leaves
from the kohlrabi, then peel.
Reserve young tender leaves, chop
finely, and add to the kohlrabi
just before the end of the cooking
time.*

1. Peel the kohlrabi and cut
into thin slices or match-
sticks. If there are any leaves,
wash them, roll up, and cut
into strips.
2. Put the kohlrabi slices and
the water into a saucepan
with a little salt. Cook, covered, over a medium heat for
about 15 minutes. Add the
leaves just before the end of
the cooking time.
3. In the meantime, thoroughly mash together the
butter and flour with a fork
to make beurre manié. Stir
this into the kohlrabi in small
lumps to thicken the liquid,
and bring to the boil. Season
with nutmeg to taste.
Delicious with hamburger or
Salisbury steak.

RED CABBAGE

SERVES 4

*Preparation and cooking
time: 1 hour 10 minutes
Kcal per portion: 235
P = 3g, F = 13g, C = 20g*

1 head red cabbage
2 tart apples
4 tbsps shortening or butter
1 small onion
2 cloves
1 cup water
½ cup dry red wine
3 sugar lumps
2 tbsps vinegar
2 tbsps cranberries

1. Remove the hard outer leaves from the cabbage. Halve the cabbage and cut out the stalk. Slice the cabbage or cut into thin strips.
2. Quarter, core, peel, and chop the apples.

> **TIP**
>
> *Red cabbage is almost always available fresh because there are early and late types. Red cabbage contains a great deal of vitamin C and is rich in iron.*

3. Heat the fat in a large saucepan and gently fry the apple pieces. Add the cabbage and the onion. Pour in the water and red wine.
4. Heat the sugar lumps in a small skillet until they caramelize. Add the vinegar and bring to the boil. Add to the cabbage mixture.
5. Tightly cover the saucepan and cook over a low heat for about 45 minutes. Finally, add the cranberries.
Serve as an accompaniment to roast pork, goose, and duck, or to game dishes.

BEETS WITH BACON

(see photo on page 34)

SERVES 4

*Preparation and cooking
time: 1 hour
Kcal per portion: 555
P = 8g, F = 51g, C = 17g*

6 raw beets (about 1½ pounds)
salt
7 slices rindless bacon
¼ stick horseradish
3 tbsps butter
⅔ cup light cream
1 tbsp red wine vinegar
1 tsp sugar
2 tbsps sour cream or plain yogurt (optional)

1. Scrub the beets thoroughly under running water; do not break the skins. Parboil in plenty of salted water for 30 minutes. Cool in cold water and remove the skins.
2. Chop the beets, not too finely, preferably in a food processor. Finely dice the bacon and finely grate the horseradish.
3. Melt the butter in a large saucepan and brown the bacon. Add the beets and cook over a medium heat, stirring occasionally.
4. Add the horseradish, cream, and salt to taste; bring back to the boil. Season with the vinegar and sugar. If desired, add sour cream or yogurt.
Serve with boiled ham, roast pork, or fish.

Peel the cooked beets.

Chop the beets, preferably in a food processor.

Add the horseradish, cream, and salt to the cooked vegetables and bring to the boil.

LEEKS WITH HAM

SERVES 4

*Preparation and cooking
time: 40 minutes
Kcal per portion: 280
P = 13g, F = 16g, C = 22g*

12 small leeks
salt and white pepper
4 slices cooked ham

**FOR THE BÉCHAMEL
SAUCE:**
2 tbsps butter
2 tbsps all-purpose flour
2 cups milk
1 egg yolk
freshly grated nutmeg

1. Cut the roots and tough green parts from the leeks, so that only the white and pale green parts remain. Wash them very thoroughly.
2. Put enough salted water to cover the leeks into a large saucepan and bring to the boil. Add the leeks and boil for 10 minutes or until almost cooked. Drain in a sieve.
3. Melt the butter for the béchamel sauce in a saucepan. Add the flour and cook gently until the mixture is pale yellow. Gradually add the milk, stirring constantly with a whisk. Bring to the boil, then remove from the heat. Stir in the egg yolk. Season with salt, white pepper, and nutmeg.
4. Heat the oven to 400°F.
5. Butter a large, shallow ovenproof dish. Wrap three leeks in each slice of ham and arrange side-by-side in the dish. Pour the sauce over them.
6. Put the leeks in the center of the oven and bake for about 15 minutes, until the top is golden-brown.
Accompaniment: mashed potato and collard greens.

STUFFED TOMATOES

SERVES 4 ■■
*Preparation and cooking
time: 1 hour
Kcal per portion: 395
P = 6g, F = 28g, C = 30g*

8 firm beefsteak tomatoes
salt and pepper
8 tbsps rice
7 tbsps olive oil
1 garlic clove
3 anchovy fillets
a few parsley sprigs
a few mint or basil leaves

*It is easy to hollow out tomatoes
using a teaspoon.*

1. Wash the tomatoes. Cut a
large slice off the tops and
reserve it. Using a teaspoon,
carefully hollow out the center. Lightly salt the insides.
2. Boil the rice in lightly salted water for 10–15 minutes.
Drain thoroughly in a sieve.
3. Press the tomato pulp
through a sieve and mix with
the rice and 4 tablespoons
of the olive oil.
4. Finely chop the garlic
clove, anchovies, and parsley. Cut the mint or basil into
thin strips. Add to the rice,
together with salt and pepper.
5. Heat the oven to 400°F.
6. Pack the rice mixture into
the tomatoes and replace
the lids.
7. Brush an ovenproof dish
with 1 tablespoon of oil. Put
the tomatoes in the dish and
brush with the remaining oil.
Bake in the center of the
oven for about 40 minutes.
Serve as an accompaniment
to fish or fish dishes. It can
also be served as a cold
appetizer with bread.

*The stuffing is made from minced
garlic, anchovy fillets, herbs, and
rice.*

*Stuff the tomatoes equally with
the seasoned rice mixture.*

SAVOY CABBAGE IN CREAM

SERVES 4 ■■
*Preparation and cooking
time: 30 minutes
Kcal per portion: 460
P = 9g, F = 43g, C = 9g*

1 Savoy cabbage (about 2½
  pounds)
salt and pepper
4 slices rindless smoked
  bacon
2 tbsps butter
1 cup sour cream or plain
  yogurt
freshly grated nutmeg

1. Remove the limp outer
leaves from the cabbage.
Cut off the stalk, quarter, and
wash the cabbage. Blanch in
boiling salted water for a few
minutes. Drain in a sieve,
then shred the leaves.
2. Finely dice the bacon.
Heat the butter in a large skillet and sweat the bacon until
the fat is transparent.
3. Add the strips of cabbage
to the diced bacon and cook
gently. Add the sour cream
or yogurt. Cover the pan and
braise the cabbage over
medium heat for 10 minutes.
4. Season with salt, pepper,
and nutmeg.
Serve as an accompaniment
to fried or broiled fish.

> **TIP**
>
> *Savoy cabbage is
> particularly
> tender when the
> new crop comes
> on to the market.
> This happens in
> May and June in
> the northeast and
> midwest, March
> and April in the
> south and
> southwest.*

POTATO BROTH

SERVES 4 ■
*Preparation and cooking
time: 40 minutes
Kcal per portions: 160
P = 6g, F = 3g, C = 27g*

1½ pounds waxy potatoes
¼ celeriac (celery root)
2 large carrots
1 leek
vegetable broth
marjoram
1 bayleaf
salt
1 tbsp chopped parsley
1 tbsp butter

1. Wash the potatoes, celeriac, and carrots. Peel the potatoes and celeriac. Scrape or
scrub the carrots. Chop the
potatoes and dice the celeriac and carrot finely. Cut off

> **TIP**
>
> *Chervil,
> marjoram, or
> chives can be
> added to the
> potato broth
> instead of
> parsley. Use
> celery if celeriac
> is not available.*

the roots and dark green
parts of the leek. Slice the
remaining parts and wash
thoroughly.
2. Put all the vegetables into
a large saucepan. Add the
broth. Add marjoram to taste
and the bayleaf. Bring to the
boil, then simmer, covered,
for 20 minutes. The potatoes
should have absorbed all the
broth and be just beginning
to fall apart.
3. Stir the parsley and butter
into the potato broth before
serving.
Serve as an accompaniment
to beef with horseradish
sauce, or serve alone as a
light vegetarian meal.

TASTY POTATO CAKES

SERVES 4 ▪
*Preparation and cooking
time: 45 minutes
Kcal per portion: 240
P = 7g, F = 13g, C = 25g*

*4 Idaho potatoes
salt
½ cup all-purpose flour
2 eggs, separated
2 tbsps light cream
freshly grated nutmeg
oil and butter for frying*

*Press the boiled potatoes through
a potato ricer.*

1. Peel and quarter the potatoes. Cook, barely covered
in salted water. Discard the
boiling water and shake the
potatoes in the saucepan
until completely dry.
2. Press the potatoes
through a potato ricer or
vegetable mill into a bowl.
Add the flour, egg yolks,

*Fold the beaten egg white into
the seasoned potato mixture.*

> **TIP**
>
> *For a change,
> add finely
> chopped herbs or
> finely diced
> onion, fried in
> butter until
> transparent, to
> the potato dough.*

*Fry the potato cakes on both
sides until golden.*

cream, salt to taste, and nutmeg. Beat the egg whites
until stiff and fold into the
mixture.
3. Heat 1 tablespoon of oil
and 1 tablespoon butter in a
large skillet. Using a spoon,
place small balls of potato
dough in the pan and press
flat. Fry until pale brown,
turn carefully, and fry the
other side until golden.
Serve as an accompaniment
to meat and game dishes, or
vegetable dishes without
meat. Can be served with
green beans as an entrée.

CREAMED POTATO WITH CRESS

SERVES 4 ▪
*Preparation and cooking
time: 30 minutes
Kcal per portion: 240
P = 6g, F = 9g, C = 34*

*2½ pounds floury potatoes
salt
1 cup milk
2 tbsps butter, cut into pieces
1 bunch garden cress
freshly grated nutmeg*

1. Peel and finely dice the
potatoes. Place in a
saucepan, just covered with
water. Add salt and boil for
15 minutes until soft.
Discard the water. Dry the
potatoes by shaking the
saucepan.
2. Heat the milk in a large
saucepan. Press the pota-
toes through a potato ricer

> **TIP**
>
> *Instead of cress,
> chopped herbs
> such as parsley
> or dill, or finely
> grated raw
> carrot, can be
> added to the
> creamed potato.*

or vegetable mill into the
milk. Whisk until the mixture
is creamy.
3. Season with salt to taste,
then stir in the butter. Finely
chop the cress with scissors
and add to the creamed
potato. Season with nutmeg.
Serve as an accompaniment
to baked fish or meat.

CREAMED POTATO AU GRATIN

SERVES 4 ▪▪
*Preparation and cooking
time: 50 minutes
Kcal per portion: 685
P = 35g, F = 45g, C = 34g*

*2½ pounds floury potatoes
salt
1 cup milk
4 tbsps butter
freshly grated nutmeg
3 eggs, beaten
2 tbsps creamed horseradish
2 cups grated Cheddar cheese*

1. Peel and finely dice the
potatoes. Put into a
saucepan, just cover with
water, add salt, and boil for
15 minutes or until soft.
2. Discard the water. Keep
the saucepan over the heat
and shake until the potatoes
are completely dry.
3. Heat the milk in a large
saucepan. Press the diced
potato through a potato
ricer or vegetable mill into
the hot milk. Whisk until the
mixture becomes creamy.
Stir in the butter in small
lumps. Season with salt and
nutmeg.
4. Add the eggs, and horseradish, and 1 cup of the
cheese to the creamed potato.
5. Butter a baking dish. Heat
the oven to 400°F.
6. Transfer the potato mixture into a piping bag. Pipe
the mixture into the baking
dish. Sprinkle with the
remaining cheese.
7. Bake in the center of the
oven for 20 minutes, or until
golden.
Serve as an accompaniment
to fried fish or meat dishes;
can also be served with
salad as a vegetarian entrée.

Dishes from Around the World

*T*hese vegetable dishes are a selection from around the world. They include native American vegetables, such as eggplant, peppers, and zucchini, turned into succulent delicacies by Mediterranean cooks, as well as ancient traditional dishes such as Swiss chard Rolls and Indian-style cabbage. All these dishes are extremely economical and nourishing and can be made all year round, thanks to the abundance of vegetables available in stores and markets.

Savoy Cabbage Indian Style
(see recipe on page 52)

45

SWISS CHARD ROLLS

SERVES 4 ■ ■

Preparation and cooking time: 1½ hours
Kcal per portion: 920
P = 32g, F = 75g, C = 30g

24 large chard leaves
2 tbsps oil
2¼ cups milk
1½ cups broth
½ Polish smoked sausage
½ cup grated yellow cheese
3 tbsps butter

FOR THE FILLING:
⅔ cup whole-wheat flour
2 eggs
salt and pepper
freshly grated nutmeg
⅓ cup water
2 slices rindless Canadian bacon
1 slice cooked ham
1 medium onion, finely diced
3 small smoked sausages
1 Polish sausage
1 bunch parsley
1 bunch Swiss chard (silverbeet) leaves
1 sprig thyme
1 sprig rosemary
½ bunch chives
2 tbsps butter

1. First prepare the filling. Put the flour into a bowl. Make a well in the center and add the eggs, salt, pepper, and nutmeg. Using a fork, mix the eggs with some of the flour.
2. Add the water, stirring with a wooden spoon. Continue beating until the mixture becomes smooth and creamy. Leave to stand for 30 minutes.
3. Meanwhile, finely dice the bacon, ham, and sausages. Finely chop the parsley, Swiss chard leaves, and remaining herbs.
4. Melt the butter in a skillet and brown the diced meat and onion. Add the herbs, stir briefly and mix thoroughly into the egg-and-flour mixture. Cool.

5. Wash the Swiss chard leaves and blanch in salted water. Drain well and spread out on a board. Place 1 tablespoon of filling on each leaf. Fold the sides of the leaves over the filling and roll up lengthwise.
6. Heat the oil in a skillet and carefully brown the rolls all over.
7. Heat the oven to 425°F.
8. Bring the milk and broth to the boil in a flameproof dish. Place the rolls side-by-side in the liquid and simmer for 15 minutes over a low heat.
9. Skin and chop the smoked sausage and sprinkle over the Swiss chard rolls. Top with the cheese and dot with butter. Brown in the center of the oven until the cheese melts.
If you cannot obtain Swiss chard leaves, large spinach or beet leaves will do.
Accompaniment: noodles or rice.
Recommended drink: a young red wine.

The filling for the rolls is made from a seasoned dough of eggs and flour, flavored with chopped herbs, onions, ham, bacon and chard leaves.

Place 1 tablespoon of the cooled filling mixture on each leaf.

Place the chard beet rolls in the milk-and-broth mixture. Sprinkle with chopped smoked sausage and grated cheese. Dot with butter and bake.

BAKED POTATOES WITH BLUE CHEESE DRESSING

SERVES 4 ■

Preparation and cooking time: 1 hour
Kcal per portion: 540
P = 14g, F = 38g, C = 34g

8 baking potatoes
2 ripe avocados
4 tbsps sour cream or plain yogurt
½ cup cottage cheese
½ blue cheese
juice of ½ lemon
3 tbsps red fish roe

1. Heat the oven to 425°F.
2. Wash the potatoes and dry with absorbent paper. Put each one on a square piece of aluminum foil. Fold the corners upward and squeeze together to enclose the potatoes.
3. Place the parcels directly on a shelf in the center of the oven for 50–60 minutes or until cooked.
4. Meanwhile halve the avocados lengthwise; pit, and peel them. Chop the flesh and purée in a liquidizer.
5. Mix the sour cream or yogurt with the cottage cheese. Mash the blue cheese with a fork and stir into the cottage cheese mixture. Stir the avocado purée into the mixture and season with the lemon juice.
6. Take the cooked potatoes out of the oven and remove the foil. Cut a cross in each potato and open out slightly. Divide the cheese mixture between the potatoes and garnish with the red roe.
Accompaniment: mixed salad.
Recommended drink: crisp, dry white wine, e.g. chablis or chardonnay.

SERBIAN-STYLE PEPPERS

SERVES 4 ■

*Preparation and cooking
time: 30 minutes
Kcal per portion: 335
P = 6g, F = 29g, C = 13g*

*2½ pounds yellow bell
   peppers
6 tomatoes
2 slices rindless smoked
   bacon
5 tbsps shortening or lard
2 large onions
1 tbsp paprika
salt*

1. Halve, core, de-seed, and wash the peppers. Slice into strips. Blanch the tomatoes in boiling water. Peel and quarter them.
2. Dice the bacon. Heat the fat in a skillet and sweat

> **TIP**
>
> *A complete main
> course dish can
> be made by
> adding slices of
> smoked dried
> sausage to the
> peppers.*

the bacon until the fat is transparent. Dice the onion, add to the pan, and brown.
3. Add the strips of pepper and tomato quarters to the skillet. Sprinkle with paprika and fry the vegetables over a low heat for 20 minutes, stirring from time to time. Season with salt to taste.
Accompaniment: rice or boiled potatoes in their skins.
Recommended drink: dry red wine.

HUNGARIAN STUFFED PEPPERS

SERVES 4 ■ ■

*Preparation and cooking
time: 1¾ hours
Kcal per portion: 465
P = 33g, F = 23g, C = 31g*

*8 large green peppers
½ cup rice
salt and pepper
1¼ pounds boneless lamb
2 small onions
1 garlic clove
1 tbsp finely chopped mint
1 tbsp finely chopped dill
1 cup broth
1 tbsp butter
⅔ cup sour cream or plain
   yogurt*

1. Cut small lids from the peppers. Carefully remove the cores and seeds, and wash the inside and outside of the peppers.
2. Pre-cook the rice in a little salted water for 5 minutes. Drain in a sieve.

>
> **TIP**
>
> *Tomato sauce,
> made from fresh
> tomatoes, can be
> poured over the
> peppers instead
> of san cream.*

3. Grind or chop the meat, onion, and garlic in a food processor. Mix with the rice and herbs. Season well with salt and pepper. Stuff the peppers with the mixture. Place upright in an ovenproof dish and cover with the lids which were removed earlier.
4. Heat the oven to 400°F.
5. Heat the butter and broth in a saucepan until the butter has melted. Pour this over the peppers. Cover the dish with a lid or foil.
6. Bake the peppers on the bottom shelf of the oven for

Grind the meat, onions, and garlic in a food processor. Mix with the rice and herbs, and season.

Put the lids back on the stuffed peppers. Place the peppers upright in an ovenproof dish or pan, close together so that they cannot fall over. Pour the butter and broth over them and bake in the oven.

60–70 minutes. Place on a serving platter and keep warm. Stir the sour cream or yogurt into the pan juices and cook until reduced to a creamy sauce. Serve with the peppers.
Accompaniment: rice.
Recommended drink: full-bodied, aromatic red wine.

MORELS WITH CREAM

SERVES 4 ■

*Preparation and cooking
time: 45 minutes
Soaking time for dried
   morels: 1 hour
Kcal per portion: 365
P = 4g, F = 33g, C = 10g*

*1¼ pounds fresh or ½ cup
   dried morels
4 tbsps butter
salt and pepper
juice of ½ lemon
1 cup sour cream or plain
   yogurt
2 tbsps brandy*

1. Soak dried morels for 1 hour; place fresh morels in cold water for 5 minutes. Wash the mushrooms thoroughly under running water to remove sand from under the wrinkled cap.
2. Halve or quarter any large mushrooms. Dry carefully with absorbent paper. Strain the soaking water from dried morels through a fine sieve into a bowl.
3. Melt the butter in a flameproof casserole. Add the mushrooms and season with salt, pepper, and lemon juice. Cook for 10 minutes over a low heat, stirring from time to time.
4. Add a little cream and, if using dried morels, the soaking water. Cook for a few minutes to reduce the liquid.
5. Add the brandy and the remaining cream. Simmer to make a thick creamy sauce. Serve as an accompaniment to fillet steak, veal cutlets, or lamb chops. Can also be used as a vol-au-vent filling.

MOUSSAKA

SERVES 4

*Preparation and cooking
time: 2 hours
Kcal per portion: 605
P = 36g, F = 45g, C = 14g*

*6 eggplants (about 2¼
    pounds)
salt and pepper
all-purpose flour
½ cup olive oil
1¼ pounds ground lamb
2 small onions
6 tomatoes
1 cup plain yogurt
3 eggs
butter for the dish*

*While the salted eggplant slices
are soaking, brown the ground
meat in hot oil, add the diced
onion and fry until transparent.*

*Arrange two layers each of
eggplants, tomatoes, and ground
meat in a baking dish. Before
browning, pour the yogurt-and-
egg sauce over them.*

1. Cut the eggplants into thin slices lengthwise. Sprinkle salt over the cut surfaces and leave 30 minutes to draw out the bitter juice.
2. Discard the juice and wash the slices. Dry them on absorbent paper and toss in flour. Heat half the olive oil in a large skillet and fry the eggplant slices in batches until pale brown.
3. Break up the ground lamb and dice the onions. Heat the remaining oil. First brown the meat, then add the diced onion, and sauté until transparent. Season with salt and pepper.
4. Blanch the tomatoes in boiling water. Peel and slice thinly.
5. Heat the oven to 400°F.
6. Butter a baking dish and cover with a third of the eggplant slices. Cover with sliced tomato and half the ground meat mixture. Then add another layer of eggplant, tomatoes, ground meat, and the remaining eggplant slices. Bake in the center of the oven for about 30 minutes.
7. Mix together the yogurt, eggs, 1 tablespoon of flour, and salt and pour this over the eggplant. Bake for a further 15 minutes or until the crust is golden-brown.
You can also use pork or beef for the ground meat.

Try using thin slices of brick cheese instead of the yogurt mixture for a quick topping.
Recommended drink:
full-bodied red wine, such as a Cabernet-Sauvignon.

RATATOUILLE

SERVES 10

*Preparation and cooking
time: 3 hours
Kcal per portion: 575
P = 6g, F = 51g, C = 18g*

*3 large Bermuda onions
3 garlic cloves
1 cup olive oil
2¼ pounds beefsteak
    tomatoes
½ cup tomato juice
½ cup dry white wine
1 bouquet garni (2 bayleaves,
    rosemary, and thyme
    sprigs, 3 parsley sprigs)
salt and pepper
2 red and 2 yellow bell
    peppers
6 eggplants
12 zucchini*

1. Slice the onions and crush the garlic cloves with the back of a knife. Blanch the tomatoes in boiling water. Peel and chop, removing the hard yellow cores.
2. Heat 4 tbsps of the oil in a large heavy skillet. Fry the onions until transparent, then add the tomatoes and garlic cloves. Pour in the tomato juice and half the white wine. Add the bouquet garni, salt, and pepper and stew over a low heat for 10 minutes.
3. Meanwhile halve, core, and de-seed the peppers. Slice into strips.
4. Wash the eggplants and zucchini, then slice thickly. Heat another 4 tbsps of oil in a saucepan. Cook these vegetables over a high heat, stirring from time to time, until golden.
5. Heat the oven to 375°F.
6. Heat the remaining oil in another saucepan and brown the sliced peppers.
7. Put all the vegetables in the saucepan with the onion-and-tomato mixture. Add the remaining wine and cover the pan.
8. Place in the center of the oven and simmer for 2 hours. Remove the vegeta-

bles, using a slotted spoon. Drain briefly (the vegetables should still be soaked in olive oil) and place in a serving dish.
This dish tastes even better the following day, whether served hot or cold.
Accompaniment:
fresh French bread.
Recommended drink:
red vin de pays or a light rosé.

> **TIP**
>
> *Preparing this ratatouille is really only worthwhile if you are catering for a large group of people. Since each vegetable must be pre-cooked individually, it takes a lot of time and effort. Ensure that you have a big enough pot to hold the entire mixture.*

GRATIN DAUPHINOIS

SERVES 4
*Preparation and cooking
time: 1 hour
Kcal per portion: 430
P = 10g, F = 28g, C = 34g*

*2¼ pounds floury potatoes
1 cup light cream
1 garlic clove
4 tbsps butter
salt and pepper
freshly grated nutmeg
¼ cup grated Swiss cheese*

1. Peel and wash the potatoes. Slice very thinly (preferably in a food processor.) Put the slices into cold water for a couple of minutes, then drain in a sieve, and dry with absorbent paper.
2. Bring the cream to the boil in a small saucepan. Cut the garlic clove in half and rub the inside of a large shallow baking dish with the cut surfaces. Grease with a third of the butter.
3. Heat the oven to 400°F.
4. Arrange a third of the sliced potato in the dish and season generously with salt,

Thinly slice the potatoes in a food processor.

Arrange potatoes, seasoning, and cheese in alternate layers in an ovenproof dish. Pour the cream over the top.

> **TIP**
>
> *If you are serving the gratin with veal or chicken, omit the cheese so that it does not overpower the delicate flavor.*

pepper, and nutmeg. Grate the cheese and sprinkle half over the potato. Arrange half the remaining potatoes on top, season again, and sprinkle with the remaining cheese.
5. Make a third layer from the remaining potato. Season with salt and pepper and pour the cream over the top.
6. Dot the dish with the remaining butter. Bake the potatoes on the bottom shelf of the oven for 45 minutes until golden. Test with a skewer to see if the potatoes are done. If not, cook for a little longer.
An accompaniment to broiled and roast meats. Can also be served as a main dish with vegetables or a colorful, mixed salad.

SAVOY CABBAGE INDIAN STYLE

(see photo on page 44)

SERVES 4
*Preparation and cooking
time: 30 minutes
Kcal per portion: 170
P = 7g, F = 12g, C = 9g*

*1 Savoy cabbage
2–3 dried red chilies
salt
3 tbsps oil
1 tsp mustard seeds
1 tbsp chickpea flour
2 tbsps minced fresh ginger
root
1 tsp turmeric
3 tbsps grated coconut*

1. Pull any limp leaves from the cabbage. Separate the remaining leaves, wash, and slice into fine strips. Wash, halve, de-seed and finely chop the chilies.
2. Bring a little salted water to the boil in a saucepan. Blanch the strips of cabbage quickly in the water, then drain in a sieve.
3. Heat the oil in a nonstick sauté pan and fry the mustard seeds briefly. Add the chickpea flour, chilies, ginger, turmeric, coconut, and cabbage.
4. Fry vigorously over a high heat for a few minutes. Then cook over a low heat for 10 minutes or until soft, stirring occasionally. Season with salt.
Accompaniment:
boiled brown rice.
Recommended drink:
mineral water or beer.

ZUCCHINI OMELETS

SERVES 4
*Preparation and cooking
time: 40 minutes
Kcal per portion: 475
P = 27g, F = 33g, C = 19g*

*6 zucchini
1 tsp salt
4 eggs
4 garlic cloves
1 bunch parsley
1 cup grated sharp Cheddar
cheese
6–8 tbsps self-rising flour
oil for frying*

1. Wash and trim the zucchini and grate them coarsely. Put into a bowl and stir in the salt and eggs.
2. Mince the garlic cloves and parsley. Add to the zucchini mixture with the cheese and sift in enough flour to make a firm dough. Mix together thoroughly.

> **TIP**
>
> *These delicate zucchini omelets with cheese make a satisfying vegetarian main dish.*

3. Heat a generous amount of oil in a large skillet. Using a spoon, put small balls of the zucchini mixture into the oil and press flat. Fry on both sides until brown and crispy. Serve immediately.
Accompaniment:
tomato salad or mixed salad. Serves 6-8 as a side dish.
Recommended drink:
crisp, white wine.

Cooking for Special Occasions

*V*egetables have become an established and highly-regarded part of cuisine. Melt-in-the-mouth vegetable flans and purées, cabbage with sparkling wine, or vegetable strudel now feature on the menus of gourmet restaurants. Distinctive fillings elevate kohlrabi, mushrooms, zucchini, and eggplant into delicacies. Delicately seasoned creamy sauces are a must with many dishes. A vegetable dish such as Stuffed Artichokes or Salsify Fritters can provide a worthy appetizer when company is invited. Vegetables offer a limitless range of possibilities, taking both leading and supporting roles in meals for special occasions.

Sauerkraut with Sparkling Wine (see recipe on page 67)

BRUSSELS SPROUT RING WITH MUSHROOM AND NUT SAUCE

SERVES 4 ■■
*Preparation and cooking
time: 45-50 minutes
Kcal per portion: 395
P = 8g, F = 36g, C = 7g*

8 ounces Brussels sprouts
4 tbsps milk
6 tbsps cream
3 egg yolks
salt and pepper

FOR THE SAUCE:
*3 tbsps butter, softened
2 tbsps ground hazelnuts
½ cup mushrooms
2 shallots
3 tbsps dry white wine
½ cup light cream
⅓ cup vegetable broth
cayenne pepper
chervil leaves to garnish*

1. Start the sauce by making a paste from 2 tablespoons of the butter and the ground nuts. Fill a large bowl with ice cubes. Place the bowl containing the nut butter inside the larger bowl and refrigerate it.
2. Heat the oven to 400°F.
3. Trim the Brussels sprouts. Steam or boil them in salted water. Cool immediately in ice-cold water. Drain and blend in a liquidizer, with the milk. Put the cream in a small saucepan and cook until reduced by half. Cool slightly, then mix with the egg yolks and stir into the Brussels sprouts purée. Season with salt and pepper.
4. Butter a tube pan and fill it with the mixture. Stand in a roasting pan half-full of hot water and cook in the oven for about 20–25 minutes.
5. Meanwhile, make the sauce. Wipe the mushrooms and dice very finely, along with the shallots. Heat the remaining tablespoon of

Fill a tube pan with the Brussels sprouts purée. Place in a water bath and bake until firm.

butter and fry the mushrooms and shallots gently. Add the wine, boil briefly, and strain through a sieve into a small saucepan. Add the cream and vegetable broth and cook until the sauce is light and creamy. Beat the ice-cold nut butter into the sauce. Season with salt, pepper, and a pinch of cayenne.
6. Carefully unmold the ring onto a serving plate. Fill the center with the mushroom-and-nut sauce. Garnish with chervil leaves.
Serve as an appetizer.
Recommended drink:
dry white wine.

> **TIP**
>
> *Broccoli or cabbage can be used instead of Brussels sprouts. The flan mixture can also be cooked in individual serving-sized molds (soufflé dishes or ramekins). Before unmolding, test the mixture with a cocktail stick to make sure it is firm.*

TOMATO-STUFFED ZUCCHINI

SERVES 4 ■■
*Preparation and cooking
time: 1 hour
Kcal per portion: 275
P = 6g, F = 23g, C = 10g*

1 cup canned tomatoes
4 medium zucchini
2 onions
3 garlic cloves
2 tbsps olive oil
1 tbsp chopped fresh
  rosemary
1 tbsp chopped fresh thyme
1 bayleaf
salt and pepper
2 tbsps black olives
1 egg
6 tbsps light cream
butter for the dish

1. Wash the zucchini. Halve lengthwise and hollow out using a teaspoon. Chop the flesh finely.
2. Drain the tomatoes and chop finely. Also chop the onions and garlic finely. Heat the olive oil in a saucepan, add all the vegetables, the rosemary, thyme, and bayleaf, and simmer for 20 minutes. Season to taste and cool.
3. Heat the oven to 350°F.
4. Chop the olives and beat the egg with the cream. Stir into the vegetables and stuff the zucchini with this mixture. Butter a shallow baking dish, arrange the zucchini in it, and bake for about 30 minutes.
Accompaniment:
crusty brown bread.
Recommended drink:
Chianti.

SHALLOTS IN MUSHROOM AND CREAM SAUCE

SERVES 6-8 ■■
*Preparation and cooking
time: 55-60 minutes
Kcal per portion (8 portions):
105
P = 3g, F = 7g, C = 7g*

1½ pounds shallots
1½ cups button mushrooms
1 tbsp butter
salt and white pepper
2 tbsps dry sherry
⅔ cup light cream
1 tbsp finely chopped chives

1. Blanch the shallots in boiling water for 2 minutes. Cool them in cold water and peel

> **TIP**
>
> *Shallots are particularly popular in French cuisine. They are milder than onions and more suitable for making delicate sauces.*

them. Place in cold salted water, bring back to the boil, and simmer for about 5 minutes.
2. Meanwhile, wipe the mushrooms and heat the butter in a saucepan. Fry the mushrooms whole, tossing to cook them evenly. Season with salt and pepper.
3. Drain the shallots into a small saucepan. Boil the liquid until reduced to about 6 tablespoons. Add the shallots to the mushrooms.
4. Add the sherry-and-shallot liquid to the vegetables and cook until completely reduced. Add the cream and continue cooking until the sauce thickens. Season with salt and pepper. Turn into a bowl, sprinkle with chives, and serve as a side-dish.

STUFFED ARTICHOKES

SERVES 4 ■■■
Preparation and cooking time: 70 minutes
Kcal per portion: 410
P = 12g, F = 35g, C = 9g

4 large globe artichokes
½ lemon
salt and pepper
⅓ cup butter
6 slices smoked salmon (lox)
2 tbsps cream
½ tsp lemon pepper
4 tbsps dry white wine
1 tbsp finely chopped shallot
3 egg yolks
a little lemon juice

1. Cut off the top third of the artichoke and snap off the stem. Rub the cut surfaces and bottoms immediately with the lemon.
2. Boil the artichokes in very lightly salted water for 30–40 minutes (depending on size.) Remove with a slotted spoon and cool. Loosen the outer leaves; remove the soft inner leaves and discard the bristly choke.
3. Generously butter four small ovenproof dishes (use about 1 tablespoon of the butter).
4. Finely chop the smoked salmon. Using the back of a spoon, squeeze the artichoke flesh out of the inner leaves, and mix it with the salmon, cream, and lemon pepper.
5. Put the wine, shallot, and a pinch of pepper into a small saucepan. Boil until only about 1 teaspoon of liquid remains.
6. Put the egg yolks into a heatproof bowl set over a pan of gently simmering water. Press the reduced wine-and-shallot mixture through a sieve into the egg yolks. Add a small knob of butter and beat over a medium heat until the sauce is creamy and sticks to the whisk.

7. Remove the bowl from the heat. Cut the rest of the butter into small pieces and stir it into the sauce. From time to time, return the bowl very briefly to the hot water, so that the butter melts completely. As soon as all the butter has been used, season the sauce with salt and lemon juice.

TIP

When buying artichokes, make sure that the heads are tightly closed and have no black spots. An artichoke should feel heavy for its size and should not look dry.

8. Place the prepared salmon mixture in the artichokes. Pour the sauce over them and brown for 1–2 minutes under a hot broiler. Serve as an appetizer.
Recommended drink: white Bordeaux.

SPINACH-STUFFED MUSHROOMS

SERVES 4 ■■
Preparation and cooking time: 50 minutes
Kcal per portion: 210
P = 6g, F = 17g, C = 4g

25 cup mushrooms
2 tbsps butter
1 cup button mushrooms
1 cup young spinach
1 bunch parsley
2 shallots
1 tsp oregano
salt and pepper
⅔ cup light cream
1 egg
6 tbsps white wine

1. Clean the open-cup mushrooms; remove and reserve the stalks. Grease a large ovenproof dish with half the butter and arrange the mushrooms in it, gills upward.
2. Wipe the button mushrooms. Wash the spinach and the parsley.
3. Chop the button mushrooms, reserved stalks, spinach, and parsley.
4. Heat the oven to 425°F.
5. Put the remaining butter in a saucepan. Finely chop the shallots and sweat until transparent. Add the mushrooms, spinach, parsley, oregano, salt, and pepper. Cook briefly, then remove from the heat.
6. Mix the egg with the cream and stir into the mixture. Spoon it into the mushrooms.
7. Sprinkle with the wine and cover the dish with aluminum foil. Cook in the oven for about 20 minutes. Serve as a starter.
Recommended drink: a light white wine such as Chardonnay.

Clean the mushrooms with a soft brush.

Carefully separate the stalks from the caps.

Place the mushrooms in a buttered ovenproof dish.

Using a teaspoon, fill the mushrooms with the spinach mixture.

SALSIFY IN PUFF PASTRY

SERVES 6 ■ ■ ■
Preparation and cooking time: 1 hour 20 minutes
Kcal per portion: 500
P = 13g, F = 35g, C = 32g

1½ pounds frozen puff dough, thawed
butter and flour for the tin
2½ pounds salsify (oyster plant)
1 tbsp lemon juice
6 slices cooked ham
2 cups broccoli flowerets
salt and pepper
1 egg yolk
4 tbsps dry white wine
⅔ cup sour cream or yogurt

1. Roll out about two-thirds of the dough to ⅛ inch thick. Butter and flour a 9-inch springform pan. Line it with the dough and refrigerate it.

> ### TIP
> *Scrub the salsify with a brush under running water and peel, using a swivel vegetable peeler. Always wear plastic or rubber gloves when peeling salsify, because the juice stains the skin.*

2. Peel the salsify and place immediately in water containing a squeeze of lemon juice, to keep it white.
3. Dice the ham. Divide the broccoli into small flowerets. Heat the oven to 425°F.
4. Cut the salsify into 2-inch pieces. Cook in salted water for 15–20 minutes, or until just soft. Drain, reserving the broth and set aside.
5. Prick the pastry base with a fork and cover with parchment paper. Add some dried beans and place in the center of the oven. After 10 minutes, reduce the heat to 375°F. After a further 5 minutes, remove the beans and the parchment paper and put the pan back into the oven.
6. Roll out a lid from the remaining dough (¼ inch larger than the pan). Decorate with left-over pastry and brush with egg yolk. Slide the lid over the pie, and bake until it changes color. The pastry should not darken too much.
7. Boil the broccoli flowerets in a little salted water for a few minutes. Remove from the water and cool in ice-cold water, so that they retain their color.
8. For the sauce, reduce 2 cups of the salsify broth by half. Blend in a liquidizer with the wine and a few pieces of salsify. Heat in a saucepan with the sour cream, but do not boil. Season with salt and pepper.
9. Add the well-drained salsify and broccoli flowerets, together with the ham, to the sauce. Reheat and pour into the pastry casing. Cover with the lid and serve immediately.

Recommended drink:
light white wine such as a Riesling.

Butter and flour a springform pan.

Roll out the puff dough and use it to line the pan.

Cover the pastry case with parchment paper, then sprinkle with dried beans.

Roll out a lid from the remaining dough and decorate with dough scraps.

SALSIFY FRITTERS

SERVES 6 ■ ■ ■
Preparation and cooking time: 1 hour 10 minutes
Kcal per portion: 330
P = 9g, F = 19g, C = 25g

⅔ cup whole-wheat flour
¾ cup dry cider
2 egg whites
2½ pounds salsify (oyster plant)
salt and pepper
1 tbsp lemon juice
oil for deep frying
lemon wedges to garnish
FOR THE SAUCE:
2 egg yolks
2 tbsps lemon juice
½ tsp Dijon mustard
1 tbsp oil
4 tbsps chopped herbs
½ cup cottage cheese
dash of Worcestershire sauce

1. Sift the flour, mix with the cider until smooth, and leave to stand for 1 hour.
2. Wash and peel the salsify. Cut into 2-inch pieces and boil in salted water with 1 tbsp of lemon juice for 15 minutes, or until soft. Cool in the liquid.
3. Make the sauce. Blend the egg yolks with the lemon juice and mustard, preferably in a liquidizer. Gradually add the oil. Add the herbs and cottage cheese. Season.
4. Whisk the egg whites with a pinch of salt until stiff, then fold into the mixture.
5. Heat the oil in a deep-fat fryer or large saucepan to 350°F.
6. Drain the salsify. Dip into the mixture and deep-fry in the oil until golden brown. Drain on absorbent paper.
7. Arrange the fritters on a serving platter, garnish with lemon wedges, and serve with the sauce.

Recommended drink:
red wine such as Cabernet Sauvignon.

KOHLRABI WITH CHANTERELLES AND CREAM CHEESE

SERVES 4
*Preparation and cooking
time: 1 hour
Kcal per portion: 315
P = 10g, F = 24g, C = 14g*

*young kohlrabi
salt and white pepper
1½ cups milk
2 shallots
1 tbsp butter
1 cup chanterelle mushrooms
1 tsp chopped marjoram
⅔ cup light cream
2 egg yolks
1 tsp cornstarch
⅓ cup cream cheese
pinch of nutmeg*

1. Peel the kohlrabi and cut into slices about ¼ inch thick. Lightly salt the milk, bring to the boil, and add the kohlrabi. Boil over a low heat for 10 minutes or until half-cooked.
2. Heat the butter in a small pan. Chop the shallots and sweat them until transparent.
3. Clean and trim the chanterelles; if large, halve lengthwise. Add to the kohlrabi and cook gently for 10 minutes.
4. Butter a gratin dish. Drain the kohlrabi and chanterelles; arrange in the dish in layers, finishing with kohlrabi.
5. Heat the oven to 375°F.
6. Mix together the marjoram, cream, egg yolks, shallots, cornstarch, and cream cheese; season with salt, pepper and nutmeg. Spread the mixture over the kohlrabi and bake for 30 minutes.
Accompaniment:
fresh crusty bread.
Recommended drink:
robust red wine.

KOHLRABI STUFFED WITH SAUSAGE

SERVES 4
*Preparation and cooking
time: 1 hour
Kcal per portion: 300
P = 11g, F = 27g, C = 4g*

*4 young kohlrabi
1 cup pork sausagemeat
2 tbsps minced parsley
salt and pepper
butter for the dish
1 cup broth
2 tbsps finely grated Cheddar
   cheese
2 tbsps butter*

1. Heat the oven to 350°F.
2. Peel and carefully hollow out the kohlrabi. Finely chop the flesh and mix with the sausagemeat and half the parsley. Season with salt and pepper.
3. Stuff the kohlrabi with this mixture. Butter an oven dish generously. Put in the kohlrabi, pour the broth over it and cover with a lid or aluminum foil.
4. Bake the kohlrabi for about 35 minutes. At the end of the cooking time remove the lid from the dish, sprinkle the kohlrabi with the cheese and dot with the butter. Return briefly to the oven, then brown under the broiler until golden.
Just before serving, sprinkle with the remaining parsley.
Accompaniment:
fresh wholemeal bread.
Recommended drink:
Burgundy or good red wine.

CREAMED CARROTS

SERVES 4
*Preparation and cooking
time: 35-45 minutes
Kcal per portion: 220
P = 3g, F = 18g, C = 13g*

*2½ pounds carrots
1 tsp sugar
⅓ cup butter
2 cups broth
2–4 tbsps light cream
salt and pepper
pinch of thyme
2 tbsps finely chopped parsley*

1. Scrub young carrots; peel older ones with a swivel peeler. Slice thinly.
2. Melt the sugar and one-third of the butter in a large saucepan. Add the carrots,

> **TIP**
>
> *The purée can be seasoned with chopped chervil. If you are using winter carrots, add a pinch of sugar.*

coat them with the butter and cook gently for 3 minutes. Add the broth and cook for 20 minutes or until very tender.
3. Drain the carrots. (Reserve the broth, which can be used to make soup.) Purée the carrots in a liquidizer, food processor, or vegetable mill.
4. Put the carrot purée in a saucepan, add the cream, and season with salt, pepper, and thyme.
5. Dice the remaining butter and stir into the hot creamed carrot. Serve sprinkled with the parsley, as a side-dish with roasts or broiled meats.

CARROTS IN VERMOUTH SAUCE

SERVES 4
*Preparation and cooking
time: 30-40 minutes
Kcal per portion: 240
P = 3g, F = 19g, C = 14g*

*2½ pounds carrots
3 tbsps butter
1 tsp sugar
2 cups broth
2 tbsps dry vermouth
⅔ cup light cream
salt and pepper
pinch of nutmeg*

1. Scrub or peel the carrots and slice thinly. Heat the butter in a large saucepan, add the carrots, and cook gently for a few minutes, stirring frequently. Add the broth, cover, and cook slowly for about 15 minutes or until slightly soft.
2. Uncover the pan and cook until all the liquid has evaporated.
3. Add the vermouth and the cream. Season with salt and

> **TIP**
>
> *Vermouth gives the sauce a distinctive touch. Serve the carrots sprinkled with chopped parsley, chives, or chervil.*

pepper and heat gently until the sauce is creamy.
Serve as a side-dish with roast meats or as part of a mixed vegetable dish.

VEGETABLE QUICHE

SERVES 6 ■■

*Preparation and cooking
time: 1 hour 5 minutes
Kcal per portion: 360
P = 8g, F = 27g, C = 22g*

*10 ounces carrots
1 head calabrese or broccoli
2-3 large mushrooms
1 small red bell pepper
3 small zucchini
salt and pepper
1 tbsp lemon juice
10 ounces frozen puff dough,
    thawed
butter for the pan
2 eggs
1 cup light cream
freshly grated nutmeg*

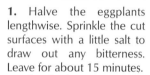

*Finely slice the individual
vegetables, preferably in a food
processor.*

*Arrange the finely sliced
vegetables in concentric rings on
the puff pastry.*

1. Scrub or peel the carrots; slice thinly. Divide the calabrese or broccoli into flow-

TIP

*Tough vegetables
should always be
pre-cooked so
that they take the
same time to
cook as other,
softer vegetables.*

erets and wipe the mushrooms. Wash and quarter the pepper; remove the core and seeds. Slice the flesh into strips. Thinly slice the zucchini.
2. Blanch the vegetables, excluding the mushrooms, in salted water for 3–4 minutes. They should still be firm.
3. Put the lemon juice in a saucepan with a little salted water and blanch the mushrooms briefly. Drain and slice thinly.
4. Butter a springform pan or quiche dish about 12 inches in diameter. Roll out the dough and use it to line the pan. Prick all over with a fork.

5. To make the custard, beat the eggs, cream, salt, pepper, and nutmeg.
6. Heat the oven to 400°F.
7. Arrange the carrot slices, overlapping, around the edge of the pastry case. Arrange the zucchini in the same way, inside the ring of carrots. Then arrange the remaining vegetables (calabrese, strips of pepper and, in the center, the mushrooms) similarly on the pastry.
8. Bake for 10 minutes. Then pour half the custard over the flan, bake for 15 minutes, then add the rest. After another 15 minutes remove the flan from the oven. Slide onto a round platter and serve immediately as a hot appetizer.
Recommended drink:
Beaujolais, mature red wine.

STUFFED EGGPLANT AU GRATIN

(see photo on page 31)

SERVES 4 ■■

*Preparation and cooking
time: 20 minutes
Kcal per portion: 260
P = 11g, F = 17g, C = 15g*

*4 medium eggplants
salt and pepper
2–3 tbsps oil
2 large tomatoes
16 basil leaves
8 slices Parma ham
6 slices Cheddar cheese*

1. Halve the eggplants lengthwise. Sprinkle the cut surfaces with a little salt to draw out any bitterness. Leave for about 15 minutes.
2. Blanch the tomatoes in boiling water, then peel and slice. Chop eight of the basil leaves into strips.
3. Heat the oven to 425°F.
4. Line a large baking sheet with aluminum foil and brush with a little oil.
5. Pat the eggplants dry thoroughly with absorbent paper and place, cut sides down, on the sheet. Bake for 20 minutes.
6. Turn the eggplants over and brush the flesh with oil. Cover each half with a slice of ham and 2 slices of tomato. Sprinkle with the basil strips and a little salt. Cover with the cheese slices and return to the oven until the cheese has melted. It should not change color.

*Halve the eggplants lengthwise
and sprinkle with salt.*

*After 15 minutes, pat the cut
surfaces dry with absorbent
paper.*

*Place the eggplants on a baking
sheet, cut surfaces downward.*

7. Arrange the eggplants on warmed plates. Garnish each half with a basil leaf, sprinkle generously with pepper, and serve as an appetizer.
Recommended drink:
red wine.

RED CABBAGE WITH RED WINE

SERVES 6–8
Preparation and cooking time: 2¼ hours
Kcal per portion (8 portions): 150
P = 3g, F = 10g, C = 7g

1 red cabbage (about 2½ pounds)
1 large onion
2 slices lean rindless bacon
5 tbsps olive oil
¾ cup red wine
1 cup broth
1 cooking apple
1 small potato
1 tsp caraway or dill seeds
pinch of sugar
salt and pepper
2 tbsps wine vinegar

1. Finely chop the red cabbage, removing the stalk. Finely dice the onion and bacon.
2. Heat the oil in a large flameproof casserole. Add the onion and bacon and sweat until the onion is transparent. Gradually add the cabbage, stirring frequently. Cook for about 15 minutes, or until it softens.
3. Add the red wine. Then add just enough broth to cover the cabbage.
4. Coarsely grate the apple and potato into the cabbage. (The apple can also be cooked whole and added to the finished dish after pressing through a sieve.) Add the caraway or dill seeds, sugar, vinegar, salt, and pepper. Cover tightly and simmer gently for about 1½ hours. At the end of the cooking time the liquid should have reduced considerably.
4. Ten minutes before serving, add the vinegar.
5. Serve as an accompaniment to chestnuts, game, poultry, or pork.

SAUERKRAUT WITH SPARKLING WINE

(see photo on page 54)

SERVES 4–6
Preparation and cooking time: 1 hour 20 minutes
Kcal per portion (6 portions): 315
P = 5g, F = 27g, C = 6g

1 onion
2 tbsps butter
1¼ pounds canned sauerkraut
¾ cup broth
1 apple
7 slices rindless smoked bacon
10 juniper berries
½ tbsp brandy (optional)
1 cup sparkling white wine

1. Finely chop the onion. Heat the butter in a large saucepan and sweat the onion until transparent. Add the sauerkraut, fry briefly and add the broth.
2. Peel and slice the apple. Chop the bacon and crush the juniper berries lightly.

> **TIP**
> *Leftover sauerkraut can be layered with ground cooked chicken and cheese sauce and baked.*

Add all to the sauerkraut, cover, and cook for at least 1 hour.
3. Thirty minutes before serving, turn the sauerkraut mixture into a sieve and drain. Return to the pan with the brandy and sparkling wine; cook until ready.
4. Serve as an accompaniment to roast game.

CHINESE-STYLE CABBAGE

SERVES 4
Preparation and cooking time: 30 minutes
Kcal per portion: 615
P = 30g, F = 47g, C = 14g

1¼ pounds lean, boneless pork
2 tbsps peanut oil
½ tsp ground ginger
salt
⅓ cup strong chicken broth
2 tbsps sake or dry sherry
2 leeks
1½ pounds Chinese (Napa) cabbage
1 tsp sugar
3 tbsps soy sauce
1 garlic clove
pinch of cayenne pepper

1. Slice the meat into thin strips. Heat 1 tablespoon of oil in a wok or deep skillet and stir-fry the meat briefly over a high heat. Season with ginger and salt. Add 2 tablespoons of chicken broth and the sake or sherry. Reduce the heat and stir-fry for a further 15 minutes.
2. Meanwhile trim and wash the leeks; slice into rings.
3. Heat 1 tablespoon of oil in another skillet and sweat the leeks for a few minutes.
4. Wash and drain the Chinese cabbage. Cut into ¾-inch strips and add to the leeks. Stir-fry until tender-crisp and remove from the pan.
5. Add the sugar, soy sauce, crushed garlic, and remaining chicken broth to the skillet and quickly bring to the boil.
6. Add the vegetables and sauce to the meat and season with cayenne.
Accompaniment:
rice.
Recommended drink:
rosé wine.

PEAS WITH HAM AND PEPPER

SERVES 4
Preparation and cooking time: 30 minutes
Kcal per portion: 175
P = 12g, F = 8g, C = 15g

4 slices cooked ham
1 small onion
1 green pepper
1 tbsp olive oil
1¾ cups thawed frozen peas
4 canned tomatoes
1 garlic clove
salt and pepper

1. Dice the ham and finely chop the onion. Halve, core and de-seed the pepper; cut into small squares.
2. Heat the olive oil in a skillet and gently cook the ham, onion, pepper, and peas for 10 minutes.

> **TIP**
> *These vegetables can be transformed into an excellent pasta dish when mixed with ⅔ cup light cream and 2 tbsps grated Parmesan. Bring to the boil and serve mixed with freshly-cooked fettuccini.*

3. Chop the tomatoes. Add to the braised vegetables, together with the crushed garlic, and cook for 5 minutes.
4. Season with salt and pepper and serve immediately as a side-dish.

Wholefood Recipes

Wholefood cuisine revels in making the most of each season's vegetables, using the right herbs and spices with each dish so that delicious aromas issue from every pot and pan. Fresh, crisp vegetables are essential, perfectly prepared so that every dish brings out each unmistakable flavor.

Why not try for yourself the Celeriac Pancakes with Tomatoes, Swiss Chard Strudel Stuffed with Vegetables and Cracked Wheat, or Mushroom Patties with Chervil Sauce. You will soon realise why wholefood cooking is becoming so popular.

Zucchini and Mushroom Terrine (see recipe on page 75)

69

BERMUDA ONIONS WITH ORIENTAL STUFFING

SERVES 4 ■■

*Preparation and cooking
time: 1½ hours
Kcal per portion: 300
P = 5g, F = 14g, C = 34g*

4 Bermuda onions
1 medium carrot
celery
butter
salt and pepper
shiitake mushrooms
1 cup strong beef broth
1 tbsp chopped fresh ginger
3 tbsps sake
2 tsps soy sauce
1½ tbsps sherry or rice wine
   vinegar
½ cup boiled basmati rice

1. Peel the onions and cut a lid from the top. Make incisions across the inside of the onion with a knife, taking

TIP

*Basmati rice has
a particularly
delicate flavor.
It takes about
20 minutes to
boil. Ordinary
long-grain rice
can be used
instead.*

care not to pierce the outer two layers of the onion. Hollow out the insides using a teaspoon, and chop finely.
2. Peel or scrub the carrot. Trim, wash, and finely dice the celery stalks.
3. Heat half the butter in a pan and lightly brown the onion, carrot, and celery. Season with salt and pepper.
4. Finely chop the mushrooms. Heat the remaining butter in a small pan, add the mushrooms, and brown them lightly. Season with salt and pepper.

*The best way to hollow out the
onions is to use a small scoop;
failing that use a teaspoon.*

*Peel or scrub the carrot and dice
it very finely.*

5. Bring the broth to the boil with the ginger, sake, soy sauce, and sherry or rice wine vinegar.
6. Heat the oven to 400°F.
7. Thoroughly mix the rice, vegetable mixture, mushrooms, and sauce. Season again with salt and pepper.
8. Butter a baking dish. Put the hollowed-out onions in the dish and stuff with the rice mixture. Cover with aluminum foil and bake for 45 minutes. After 30 minutes, uncover and continue cooking until the onions are tender.

CHEESE-TOPPED SPINACH DUMPLINGS

SERVES 4 ■■

*Preparation and cooking
time: 45 minutes
Kcal per portion: 415
P = 29g, F = 29g, C = 9g*

6 cups spinach
salt and pepper
1 cup cottage cheese
3 egg yolks
2–3 tbsps whole-wheat flour
freshly grated nutmeg
1 cup grated Cheddar cheese
butter for the dish

1. Carefully sort the spinach and wash thoroughly. Bring a saucepan of well-salted water to the boil. Blanch the spinach for 1 minute, then drain in a colander. Squeeze out well and chop finely.
2. Put the cottage cheese into a bowl and mix thoroughly with the spinach, egg yolks, and enough flour to make a firm dough. Season well with salt, pepper, and nutmeg.
3. Bring a large saucepan of well-salted water to the boil and heat the broiler. Butter a large heatproof dish.
4. Using a spoon, make dumplings from the spinach mixture and cook for 2–3 minutes in the gently boiling salted water. Remove, using a slotted spoon. Drain and place side-by-side in the dish. Sprinkle with cheese and brown quickly under the broiler.
Serve as an accompaniment to fish dishes or as a hot snack served with a cheese sauce.

EGGPLANT AU GRATIN

SERVES 4 ■

*Preparation and cooking
time: 45 minutes
Kcal per portion: 485
P = 22g, F = 38g, C = 11g*

2 medium eggplants (about
   1½ pounds)
salt and white pepper
6 tbsps olive oil
4 large beefsteak tomatoes
2 tbsps chopped basil leaves
1 tsp oregano
8 ounces mozzarella cheese

1. Wash the eggplants and remove the stalk ends. Cut lengthwise into slices about ½ inch thick. Sprinkle with salt and leave to stand for 15 minutes.
2. Blanch the tomatoes. Peel and cut into thick slices.
3. Heat the oven to 400°F.
4. Squeeze out the eggplant slices thoroughly and dry on absorbent paper. Heat 4 tablespoons of oil in a nonstick skillet. Quickly brown the eggplant slices on both sides. Place side-by-side on a baking sheet.
5. Cover the eggplant slices with the tomato slices. Sprinkle with salt, pepper, basil, and oregano. Thinly slice the mozzarella and lay on top. Drizzle with the remaining olive oil and bake in the center of the oven for 15 minutes. Heat the broiler and quickly brown the eggplant.
An accompaniment to fish dishes or a hot appetizer.
Recommended drink:
a light, aromatic red wine.

RED LENTILS IN RICE PAPER

SERVES 4 ■■
*Preparation and cooking
time: 1 hour
Soaking time: a few hours
Kcal per portion: 360
P = 15g, F = 19g, C = 29g*

1 cup split red lentils
1 tsp turmeric
4 sheets rice paper
1 red onion, finely diced
2 garlic cloves
2 tbsps grated fresh ginger
   root
1 green chili
2 tbsps oil
1 cup broth (beef, chicken, or
   vegetable)
2 tbsps dry sherry
2 tbsps sherry vinegar
2 tbsps soy sauce
salt and pepper
pinch of cumin
½ cup plain yogurt
oil for the dish
1 egg yolk

*Soak the sheets of rice paper in
cold water until they turn milky
white.*

*Before baking, brush the parcels
with beaten egg yolk.*

1. Cook the lentils with the turmeric in a generous amount of water until tender (about 30 minutes). Drain thoroughly in a sieve.
2. Soak the sheets of rice paper in cold water until they turn milky white. Remove carefully and spread them out next to one another on a kitchen towel.
3. Peel the garlic and ginger. Core and de-seed the chili. Dice all three finely.
4. Heat the oil in a flame-proof casserole and lightly brown the garlic, ginger, and chili. Add the lentils and pour in the broth, sherry, vinegar, and soy sauce.
5. Season with salt, pepper, and a pinch of cumin. Cook over a medium heat until almost all the liquid has evaporated, then remove from the heat and stir in the yogurt.
6. Heat the oven to 400°F.
7. Spread the lentil mixture over the rice paper. Fold the side edges over the filling, then fold lengthwise. Butter a baking sheet and put the parcels on it. Brush with beaten egg yolk and bake in the center of the oven for 10 minutes or until golden. Serve as a starter.
Recommended drink:
white wine or fruit juice.

CHEESE-TOPPED LENTIL PATTIES

SERVES 4 ■
*Preparation and cooking
time: 30 minutes
Kcal per portion: 715
P = 30g, F = 55g, C = 24g*

1 small leek
2 medium carrots (about 7
   ounces)
5–6 tbsps oil
⅔ cup cooked lentils
2 tbsps chopped walnuts
½ cup sour cream or plain
   yogurt
2 eggs
salt and pepper
1 cup grated Cheddar cheese

1. Cut the roots and dark green parts from the leek. Halve the leek lengthwise and wash thoroughly in running water. Peel or scrub the carrots. Finely dice both vegetables.
2. Heat 2 tablespoons of the oil in a flameproof casserole. Gently fry the vegetables, then stir in the lentils. Remove from the heat and cool the mixture.
3. When cool, stir in the walnuts, sour cream or yogurt, and eggs. Season with salt and pepper, and shape into small patties.
4. Heat the broiler to high.
5. Heat the remaining oil in a nonstick skillet. Fry the patties for about 2 minutes on each side over a medium heat.
6. Drain the patties on absorbent paper. Put them on a heatproof plate. Sprinkle with grated cheese and brown under the broiler.
Accompaniment:
mixed salad and cheese sauce flavored with herbs.
Recommended drink:
a light white wine.

CELERIAC PANCAKES WITH TOMATOES

SERVES 4 ■
*Preparation and cooking
time: 30 minutes
Kcal per portion: 460
P = 21g, F = 36g, C = 12g*

1 large celeriac (about 14
   ounces)
2 tbsps milk
3 eggs
3 tbsps whole-wheat flour
2 tbsps chopped hazelnuts or
   walnuts
salt and pepper
freshly grated nutmeg
4–6 tbsps oil
4 small firm tomatoes
⅔ cup grated Parmesan
   cheese

1. Peel the celeriac and grate it coarsely. Add the milk and eggs, then stir in the flour and nuts. Mix well and season with salt, pepper, and nutmeg.
2. Line a baking sheet with nonstick baking paper.
3. Heat a little oil in a nonstick skillet. Using a ladle, pour in a little of the celeriac mixture. Swirl evenly over the pan and fry on both sides until brown. Make the remaining mixture into pancakes in the same way. Place the cooked pancakes on the lined baking sheet.
4. Heat the broiler to high.
5. Slice the tomatoes. Arrange on top of the pancakes and sprinkle with cheese. Quickly brown under the broiler.
The pancakes are also excellent made with zucchini or cauliflower.
Serve as an accompaniment to meat dishes.

CRACKED WHEAT AND ZUCCHINI PATTIES

SERVES 4 ■■
Preparation and cooking time: 50 minutes
Kcal per portion: 580
P = 19g, F = 22g, C = 77g

1¼ pounds zucchini
salt and pepper
1 cup cracked wheat
4 slices whole-wheat bread
bunch of green onions (scallions)
2 garlic cloves
½ tsp rosemary
1 tsp thyme
2 eggs
breadcrumbs
4–5 tbsps oil

The best way to grate zucchini is in a food processor.

1. Trim the ends off the zucchini, wash, and coarsely grate them. Sprinkle with salt and leave to stand for 30 minutes.
2. Cook the cracked wheat in a pressure cooker, covered in water, for 15 minutes. Soak the slices of bread in lukewarm water.

Finely slice the green onions, including some of the green parts.

> ### TIP
>
> *If you do not have a pressure cooker, it is better to soak the cracked wheat in cold water for a few hours, then boil it in a saucepan for 25–30 minutes until tender but still firm.*

3. Trim and wash the green onions. Slice finely, including some of the green parts. Finely chop the garlic.
4. Squeeze out the zucchini and slices of bread thoroughly. Put into a bowl. Thoroughly drain the cracked wheat in a sieve.

Fry the patties in oil on both sides for 3–4 minutes.

Add to the zucchini and bread, together with the green onion, garlic, and herbs. Gradually add the eggs. Season with salt and pepper and work into a soft dough. If it is too wet, bind with breadcrumbs.
5. Heat the oil in a nonstick skillet. Fry the patties over a medium heat for 3–4 minutes on each side.
Accompaniment: cheese sauce.

BERMUDA ONIONS WITH SOUFFLÉ STUFFING

SERVES 2 ■■
Preparation and cooking time: 1½ hours
Kcal per portion: 730
P = 47g, F = 48g, C = 28g

4 Bermuda onions
butter for the dish

FOR THE STUFFING:
⅔ cup light cream
1 cup cottage cheese
½ cup grated Parmesan cheese
3 eggs, separated
salt and white pepper
freshly grated nutmeg

1. Heat the oven to 400°F. Bake the onions, un-peeled, for 1 hour.
2. Cool and peel the onions. Cut a lid from the top and hollow out the center, leaving three layers of onion intact. Butter an ovenproof dish and put the onions in it.
3. For the stuffing, blend the onion flesh and the cream in a liquidizer. Press through a sieve and mix with the cottage cheese, Parmesan, and egg yolks. Season with salt and pepper. Whisk the egg whites stiffly and fold into the mixture. Stuff the onions and bake in the center of the oven for 15 minutes.
Makes a good accompaniment to any meat dish and a delicious appetizer.

ZUCCHINI AND MUSHROOM TERRINE

(see photo on page 68)

SERVES 4 ■■
Preparation and cooking time: 1 hour 20 minutes
Kcal per portion: 460
P = 14g, F = 40g, C = 13g

1¼ pounds zucchini
2 cups mushrooms
2 small shallots
3 tbsps butter
1 cup light cream
1 cup milk
4 eggs
bunch of parsley
salt and white pepper
freshly grated nutmeg

1. Wash the zucchini, trim, and slice thinly. Wipe the mushrooms and slice thinly. Finely dice the shallots.
2. Heat the butter in a flameproof casserole and lightly brown the vegetables.
3. Heat the oven to 400°F.
4. Thoroughly whisk together the cream, milk, and eggs. Mince the parsley, add to the mixture, and season with salt, pepper, and nutmeg. Add the vegetables. Butter a 1½-quart terrine mold (or line with parchment paper) and fill with the mixture. Bake in the center of the oven for about 45 minutes.
The terrine looks very attractive if it is made in a round mold and covered with slices of lightly cooked zucchini after unmolding.
Excellent hot or cold.
Recommended drink: strong, full-bodied white wine.

SWISS CHARD STRUDEL STUFFED WITH VEGETABLES AND CRACKED WHEAT

SERVES 4 ■ ■

Preparation and cooking time: 1 hour 10 minutes
Kcal per portion: 420
P = 21g, F = 20g, C = 39g

1 cup cracked wheat
3 cups diced mixed
  vegetables (leeks, carrots,
  zucchini, kohlrabi)
10 large chard leaves
salt and white pepper
2 shallots
2 tbsps butter
freshly grated nutmeg
1 cup cottage cheese
4 eggs

1. Cook the cracked wheat, covered in water, in a pressure cooker for 15 minutes. Discard the water and drain.
2. Trim and wash the vegetables and cut into fine strips. Separate the chard stalks from the leaves. Finely slice the stalks and add to the other vegetables.
3. Bring a generous amount of salted water to the boil. First blanch the mixed vegetables for 2 minutes, then the chard leaves for 30 seconds. Drain the leaves. Spread them out next to each other, slightly overlapping, on a large piece of greased aluminum foil.
4. Dice the shallots finely. Heat the butter in a large skillet, add the onion, and sweat until transparent. Add the drained vegetables. Cook for a few minutes, then season with salt, pepper, and nutmeg.
5. In a bowl, mix the cottage cheese with the eggs. Add the cracked wheat and the vegetables. Mix well and season generously.
6. Spread the mixture over the chard leaves and roll the

Spread the Swiss chard out on a large piece of aluminum foil, with the leaves just overlapping.

Spread the cheese mixture evenly over the chard leaves.

Wrap the chard leaf strudel tightly in aluminum foil.

leaves up like a jellyroll. Wrap tightly in the aluminum foil and cook in lightly simmering salted water for 15 minutes. Serve hot, cut into thick slices.
Accompaniment:
sherry or port wine sauce.

BRUSSELS SPROUT LEAVES IN CREAMY SAUCE

SERVES 4 ■

Preparation and cooking time: 30 minutes
Kcal per portion: 340
P = 6g, F = 31g, C = 8g

1¼ pounds Brussels sprouts
salt and white pepper
1 cup light cream
3 tbsps white port
4 tbsps butter
freshly grated nutmeg

1. Trim and wash the Brussels sprouts. Separate the individual leaves. Bring a large amount of salted water to the boil and blanch the leaves for about 1 minute. Drain in a sieve.
2. Bring the cream, port, and butter to the boil in a sauté pan or shallow flameproof casserole. Season with salt, pepper, and nutmeg, and cook until reduced a little.
3. Put the Brussels sprout leaves into the cream sauce and toss gently. Serve immediately.
Serve as an accompaniment to white meat, poultry, and game dishes.

> **TIP**
>
> *Use fairly large sprouts for this dish. The firmer and more tightly closed the sprouts, the better they are.*

CHARD TOPPED WITH PARMESAN

SERVES 4 ■

Preparation and cooking time: 30 minutes
Kcal per portion: 310
P = 14g, F = 27g, C = 3g

12 large chard leaves
½ cup beef broth
cream
salt and pepper
freshly grated nutmeg
⅔ cup grated Parmesan
  cheese
2 egg yolks

1. Wash the chard leaves. Cut out the stalks and slice both the stalks and the leaves into thin strips, keeping them separate.
2. Bring the broth to the boil in a flameproof casserole and briefly poach the chard stalks. Add just under half

> **TIP**
>
> *Swiss chard stalks and leaves take very different times to cook, so always cook the stalks first, then just heat the leaves.*

the cream and simmer until reduced by a third. Add the leaf strips and cook for about 1 minute. Season with salt, pepper, and nutmeg.
3. Heat the broiler to high.
4. Put the chard mixture into an ovenproof dish and sprinkle with a thick layer of Parmesan. Whisk the egg yolks with the remaining cream and pour evenly over the cheese. Brown quickly under the broiler.
Serve as an accompaniment to poultry and game.

MUSHROOM PATTIES WITH CHERVIL SAUCE

SERVES 4 ■■
Preparation and cooking time: 45 minutes
Kcal per portion: 640
P = 13g, F = 56g, C = 21g

FOR THE PATTIES:
1 Bermuda onion
2 cups mushrooms
oil for frying
½ cup cooked oatmeal
2 tbsps chopped flat-leaved parsley
3 eggs
salt and white pepper
whole-wheat flour if needed

FOR THE SAUCE:
1 cup broth (vegetable, beef or chicken)
⅔ cup light cream
4 tbsps butter
salt and white pepper
2 tbsps whipped cream
4 tbsps chopped fresh chervil

1. Finely dice the onion. Wipe or peel the mushrooms and finely dice.
2. Heat 2 tablespoons of oil in a skillet. Gently sweat the onion without allowing it to turn color.
3. Combine the onions, mushrooms, oatmeal, and parsley in a bowl. Gradually add the eggs. Season with salt and pepper and work into a soft dough. If it is too soft, add a little whole-wheat flour.
4. For the sauce, heat the broth, cream, and butter in a saucepan. Season with salt and pepper, and cook until reduced by a third.
5. Make small patties from the mushroom mixture. Heat 4–6 tablespoons oil in a nonstick skillet. Fry the patties for 3–4 minutes on each side.
6. Meanwhile finely chop the chervil, reserving a few springs to garnish. Beat the reduced sauce with a hand-held mixer, adding the

If liked, peel the mushrooms, using a pointed knife.

Just before serving, mix the whipped cream and chervil into the sauce.

whipped cream and chopped chervil. Pour the sauce over the patties and garnish with chervil.
Accompaniment:
glazed carrots or broccoli flowerets.

ASPARAGUS AND WHOLE-WHEAT GRAINS TOPPED WITH PARMESAN

SERVES 4 ■■
Preparation and cooking time: 45 minutes
Kcal per portion: 455
P = 23g, F = 28g, C = 36g

4½ pounds asparagus
salt and white pepper
1 tsp sugar
2 tbsps butter
1 tbsp chopped shallot
⅔ cup cooked whole-wheat berries
1 cup grated Parmesan cheese
⅔ cup light cream
2 egg yolks

1. Scrape the asparagus stalks and cut off the lower ends if necessary. Bring a generous amount of salted, sugared water to the boil. Boil the spears for 5-10 minutes, depending on thickness, until still firm. Drain well.
2. Heat the butter in a skillet. Gently fry the shallot and whole-wheat grains. Season with salt and pepper.
3. Heat the broiler to high.
4. Transfer the asparagus spears to an ovenproof dish. Sprinkle first with whole-wheat grains, then with Parmesan.
5. Beat the cream with the egg yolks and pour this over the cheese. Quickly brown the asparagus under the broiler.
Recommended drink:
Burgundy or Cabernet Sauvignon.

LEEKS TOPPED WITH GORGONZOLA

SERVES 4 ■■
Preparation and cooking time: 45 minutes
Kcal per portion: 375
P = 15g, F = 31g, C = 10g

4 young leeks
salt and white pepper
1 medium carrot
2 tbsps butter
½ cup light cream
freshly grated nutmeg
⅔ cup Gorgonzola cheese
2 egg yolks
butter for the dish

1. Trim off the roots, remove and reserve the green parts from the leeks. Cut in half, wash thoroughly and blanch in boiling salted water for about 3 minutes. Remove and drain well.
2. Trim, wash, and finely dice the carrot, together with the green parts of the leeks. Heat the butter in a flame-proof casserole and sweat the diced vegetables. Season with salt and pepper.
3. Heat the oven to 400°F.
4. Bring the cream, salt, pepper, and nutmeg to the boil in a saucepan. Press the Gorgonzola through a sieve into the cream. Bring back to the boil, then remove from the heat and beat in the egg yolks.
5. Butter an ovenproof dish and add the leeks. Cover with the diced vegetables. Pour over the cream and bake in the center of the oven for about 15 minutes or until cooked.
Serve as an accompaniment to roast beef or veal.

COTTAGE CHEESE AND VEGETABLE STRUDEL

SERVES 4 ■ ■ ■
*Preparation and cooking
time: 50 minutes
Relaxing time: 2 hours
Kcal per portion: 1085
P = 41g, F = 77g, C = 56g*

FOR THE DOUGH:
*2½ cups whole-wheat flour
pinch of salt
1 egg
1 egg yolk
⅔ cup sour cream or yogurt
6 tbsps butter
1 egg yolk
4 tbsps light cream*

FOR THE FILLING:
*1 kohlrabi
2 carrots
4 zucchini
2 cups cottage cheese
4 eggs
2 tbsps chopped kohlrabi
    leaves
2 tbsps chopped carrot leaves
½ cup roast pistachio nuts
white pepper
freshly grated nutmeg*

1. To make the dough, sift the flour and salt on to the work top. Make a well in the center. Place the egg, egg yolk, and cream in the well. Dot the butter, in small knobs, around the edge. Using a round-bladed knife, first cut the fat into the flour. Quickly knead to a smooth dough, working from the outside inwards. Wrap in foil and chill for 2 hours.
2. For the filling, peel the kohlrabi and carrot. Cut the ends from the zucchini. Chop everything into thin sticks. Blanch in plenty of boiling salted water and drain thoroughly in a sieve.
3. Put the cottage cheese into a bowl. Stir until smooth and gradually add the eggs, chopped kohlrabi, and carrot leaves, pistachio nuts, and drained vegetables.

Season with salt, pepper and nutmeg.
4. Heat the oven to 400°F.
5. Roll out the dough on a floured board into as thin a square as possible. Cover with the cheese-and-vegetable mixture and roll up like a jellyroll.

> ### TIP
> *The strudel can be served either as a side-dish or as a main course, possibly with an herb-flavored sauce. Toasted sunflower seeds can be added to the cheese mixture instead of roasted pistachio nuts.*

6. Butter a baking sheet and put the strudel on it, seam downward. Warm the egg yolks and cream but do not let the mixture boil. Brush the strudel with the mixture. Bake in the center of the oven for 15–20 minutes until golden.
Recommended drink:
a dry Sylvaner.

Put the cheese, eggs, pistachio nuts, and chopped leaves into a bowl and stir.

Stir the vegetables into the cheese mixture.

Spread the cheese and vegetable mixture over the rolled-out dough.

Before baking, brush the strudel with a mixture of warmed egg yolk and cream.

BAKED POTATOES WITH MUSHROOM FILLING

SERVES 4 ■
*Preparation and cooking
time: 1 hour 10 minutes
Kcal per portion: 345
P = 7g, f = 24g, C = 25g*

*4 large floury potatoes
1 cup mushrooms
1 shallot
3 tbsps butter
⅔ cup yogurt or sour cream
salt and white pepper
⅔ cup fresh beansprouts*

1. Heat the oven to 400°F. Wash the potatoes throughly and wrap, unpeeled, in aluminum foil. Bake for about 1 hour, until cooked.
2. Meanwhile, wipe and finely chop the mushrooms;

> ### TIP
> *The potatoes look attractive served in the open aluminum foil. In summer, the potato parcels can also be barbecued.*

finely dice the shallot. Heat the butter in a skillet, add the mushrooms and shallot, and brown lightly over a medium heat. Stir in the yogurt. Season with salt and pepper, and bring to the boil. Add the beansprouts and heat quickly in the mushroom sauce.
3. Take the potatoes out of the oven. Unwrap and cut off a lid. Hollow out the potatoes a little and fill with the mushroom mixture.

Quick-and-easy Recipes

*T*he quick recipes in this chapter are proof that there's no magic about fast food. Barely half an hour is all that's needed to produce an attractively served vegetable side-dish or main course. Eggplant with Garlic, Curried Chinese Cabbage with Almonds, Cheese-topped Fennel with a Nut Crust – these all can become complete meals for those who are happy not to eat meat, particularly when complemented by a bowl of salad or a nourishing dessert. If time is short, frozen vegetables can be used instead of fresh ones, making the preparation and cooking times even quicker.

Eggplant with Garlic
(see recipe on page 84)

EGGPLANT WITH GARLIC

(see photo on page 83)

SERVES 4
Preparation and cooking time: 30 minutes
Kcal per portion: 225
P = 3g, f = 19g, C = 10g

1½ pounds eggplant
5 tbsps olive oil
4 garlic cloves
2 cups canned chopped
   tomatoes
salt and pepper
2 tsps thyme, fresh or dried

1. Wash the eggplants and remove the stalk ends. First quarter lengthwise, then cut into slices about ½ inch thick. Heat the olive oil in a large skillet and fry until golden. Remove from the pan.
2. Crush the garlic and stir into the oil remaining in the pan. Sweat until golden.

> **TIP**
>
> *This vegetable dish also tastes delicious cold. It could then be seasoned with a little red wine vinegar or lemon juice.*

3. Add the tomatoes and cook over a high heat until reduced by a third.
4. Return the eggplants to the skillet. Season with salt, pepper, and thyme and cook for a further 10 minutes.
For a complete meal, add 2 cups ground beef and serve with potatoes.
Can be served as an accompaniment to leg of lamb or roast chicken.

CAULIFLOWER WITH HAZELNUT BUTTER

SERVES 4
Preparation and cooking time: 30 minutes
Kcal per portion: 385
P = 6g, F = 38g, C = 6g

1 medium cauliflower (about
   1½ pounds)
salt and pepper
juice of ½ lemon
⅔ cup butter
5 tbsps ground nuts
freshly grated nutmeg

1. Remove any leaves from the cauliflower, divide it into the smallest possible flowerets and wash.
2. Bring a generous amount of water, seasoned with salt and lemon juice, to the boil. Add the cauliflower flowerets, bring to the boil, then simmer for 8 minutes, until still firm.
3. Melt the butter in a flameproof casserole. Sprinkle in the ground nuts and cook until the butter foams. Season with salt, pepper, and nutmeg.
4. Using a slotted spoon, remove the cauliflower from the cooking liquid and drain thoroughly. Arrange on a plate and pour the hot nut butter over it. Serve immediately.
Almonds, walnuts, pistachio nuts, or hazelnuts can be used.
Gorgonzola cream sauce also goes very well with cauliflower, instead of the nut butter.

CURRIED CHINESE CABBAGE WITH ALMONDS

SERVES 4
Preparation and cooking time: 25 minutes
Kcal per portion: 195
P = 6g, F = 14g, C = 11g

1 large onion
2 tbsps oil
1 head Chinese (Nappa)
   cabbage
3 garlic cloves
salt and pepper
2 tbsps curry powder
3 cups canned tomatoes
2 tbsps flaked almonds
15g/½oz butter
1 bunch coriander (cilantro)
   or flat-leaved parsley

1. Chop the onion. Heat the oil in a large skillet and sweat the onion until transparent.
2. Meanwhile quarter the Chinese cabbage lengthwise, remove the stalk, and slice across into ¼-inch strips. Wash and drain well.
3. Crush the garlic, add to the chopped onion, and sweat briefly. Add the Chinese cabbage. Cook, covered, for 3 minutes.
4. Season the vegetables with salt and pepper. Sprinkle with the curry powder. Add the tomatoes, together with the juice. Cover and cook for 10 minutes over a low heat.
5. Meanwhile, heat the butter in a nonstick skillet and stir-fry the almonds until golden.
6. Rinse the coriander or parsley, pull off the leaves, pat dry, and just before serving, sprinkle them over the curried Chinese leaves together with the almonds.
Accompaniment:
rice, preferably a mixture of long-grain and wild rice.
Recommended drink:
buttermilk.

BROCCOLI WITH HAM HOCKS

SERVES 4
Preparation and cooking time: 25 minutes
Kcal per portion: 175
P = 14g, F = 12g, C = 2g

3 cups broccoli, fresh or
   frozen
salt and pepper
1 tbsp oil
1 medium onion
7 thick slices ham hocks
freshly grated nutmeg

1. Trim fresh broccoli, divide into flowerets and wash. Slice the stalks. Thaw frozen broccoli and cut into small flowerets.
2. Bring a large saucepan of salted water to the boil and cook the broccoli for 7 minutes so that it is still firm.

> **TIP**
>
> *Without the pork, the broccoli also makes a good sidedish with fish and poultry. The pork can be replaced by shrimp and the vegetables served with fish dishes.*

Cool in ice-cold water and drain well.
3. Meanwhile heat the oil in a large sauté pan. Chop the onion and sweat until transparent.
4. Finely dice the pork. Add to the pan with the broccoli. Season with salt, pepper, and nutmeg. Cover, and cook for a further 7 minutes. Serve with meat balls or potato pancakes.

CHARD IN RED WINE VINEGAR

SERVES 4
Preparation and cooking time: 25 minutes
Kcal per portion: 155
P = 4g, F = 13g, C = 6g

6 cups Swiss chard
butter
3 garlic cloves
salt and pepper
generous pinch of cayenne
4 tbsps sour cream or plain yogurt
1 tbsp red wine vinegar

Cut off the end of the Swiss chard stalks.

1. Wash the Swiss chard and cut off the end of the stalks. Cut or pull the leaves from the stalks. Slice the stalks into ½ inch strips.

> **TIP**
>
> *Chard makes a good starter, either hot or cold.*

Cut out the hard leaf end.

2. Heat the butter in a large skillet. Add the stalk strips and sweat, covered, over a low heat for 8 minutes.
3. Crush the garlic, and add to the stalks. Stir in the chard leaves. Season with salt, pepper, and cayenne.
4. Add the sour cream or yogurt and vinegar. Stir and bring to the boil.
The vegetables can be sprinkled with toasted pinenuts (pignolas) or grated Parmesan.

Accompaniment:
serve with poached eggs and mashed potato sprinkled with lots of chives. Also tasty with Smithfield ham or cold roast beef.

Slice the Swiss chard stalks into ½-inch strips.

First sweat the tender stalk strips in butter over a low heat. Then stir in the green leaves.

CREAMY LEEKS TOPPED WITH CHEESE

SERVES 4
Preparation and cooking time: 30 minutes
Kcal per portion: 460
P = 19g, f = 39g, C = 9g

8 large leeks
salt and white pepper
butter for the dish
freshly grated nutmeg
1 cup cottage cheese
1 cup light cream
6 tbsps grated Dutch cheese
3 tbsps sunflower seeds

1. Trim the leeks and cut off the ends. Slit lengthwise and rinse well under cold running water.
2. Heat the oven to 475°F.
3. Cut the leeks diagonally into ½ inch pieces. Blanch for 3 minutes in boiling salted water. Cool in ice-cold water and drain well in a sieve.
4. Butter a large shallow baking dish and arrange the leeks in it. Season with salt, pepper, and nutmeg.
5. In a bowl, mix together the cottage cheese, cream, grated cheese, and sunflower seeds. Season with salt, pepper, and nutmeg; spread over the leeks. Bake in the center of the oven for 15 minutes until golden.

Accompaniment:
mashed potato with lots of chives. Serves 8 as a starter, browned in individual dishes.
Recommended drink:
white wine spritzer.

CHEESE-TOPPED FENNEL WITH A NUT CRUST

SERVES 2
Preparation and cooking time: 30 minutes
Kcal per portion: 1145
P = 37g, F = 98g, C = 29g

6 fennel bulbs
salt and pepper
butter for the dish
1 cup sour cream or plain yogurt
⅔ cup grated Gouda cheese
1 cup ground walnuts
freshly ground black pepper

1. Wash the fennel bulbs. Cut off and reserve any leaves. Cut the bulbs lengthwise into slices about ½ inch thick.
2. Cook the fennel in boiling salted water for 3 minutes. Remove using a slotted spoon and drain well.
3. Heat the oven to 425°F.
4. Butter a large ovenproof dish and arrange the fennel slices so that they overlap.
5. Put the sour cream or yogurt into a bowl. Add the cheese and nuts and mix together. Season well with salt and pepper. Spread evenly over the fennel.
6. Bake in the center of the oven for 15 minutes, or until golden. Sprinkle with reserved fennel leaves.
This dish can be made more substantial by sandwiching well-mashed canned tuna between the fennel slices.

Accompaniment:
French bread or mashed potato.
Recommended drink:
light white wine.

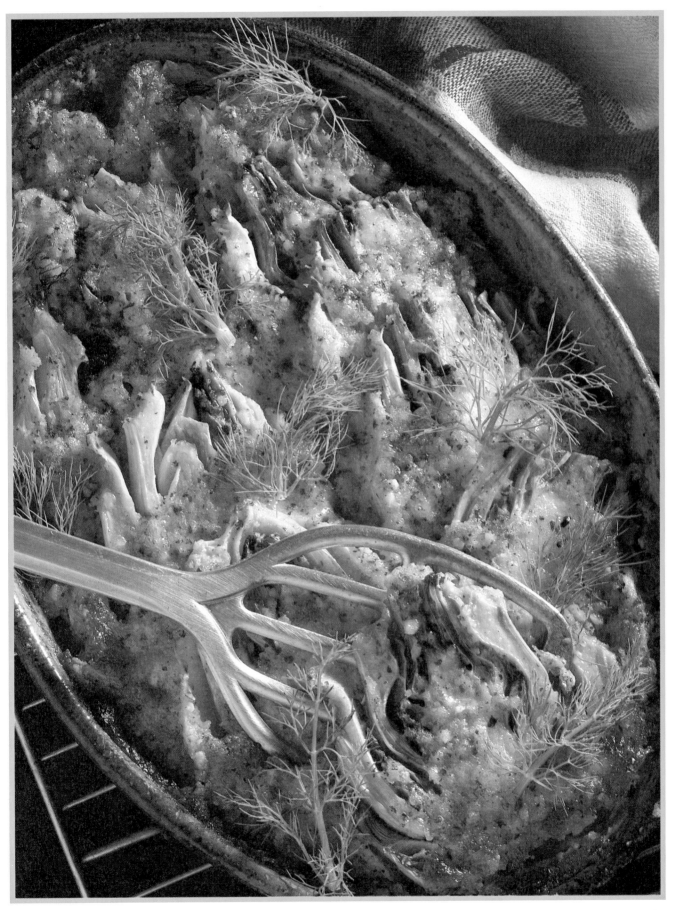

BRAISED ASPARAGUS IN CHERVIL SAUCE

SERVES 2
Preparation and cooking time: 30 minutes
Kcal per portion: 380
P = 15g, F = 30g, C = 18g

2½ pounds asparagus
3 tbsps butter
salt and white pepper
juice of 1 lemon
2 tbsps maple syrup
8 tbsps chopped chervil
2 egg yolks
1¼ cups plain yogurt

1. Scrape the lower part of the asparagus stalks and cut off the ends. Cut the stalks diagonally into pieces about 1½ inches long. Set the tips to one side.
2. Heat the butter in a large skillet. Sweat the asparagus, covered, without the tips, for 15 minutes over medium heat. After 5 minutes, add salt and pepper. Drizzle with lemon juice and maple syrup.
3. Meanwhile, rinse the chervil, pat dry, and snip off the stalks. Reserve a few sprigs for garnishing. Blend the remaining chervil in a liquidizer with the egg yolks and yogurt, to make a smooth sauce. Season with salt and pepper.
4. About 5 minutes before the end of the cooking time, add the asparagus tips to the skillet.
5. Arrange the asparagus on four warmed plates, with a tablespoon of sauce in the center. Garnish with chervil leaves.
Accompaniment: new potatoes. This quantity serves four as a sidedish and is tasty with poached salmon.
Recommended drink: claret.

STIR-FRIED ASPARAGUS

SERVES 4
Preparation and cooking time: 30 minutes
Kcal per portion: 315
P = 7g, f = 28g, C = 8g

1¼ pounds asparagus
2 cups snow peas
salt
3 tbsps oil
3 tbsps sesame seeds
3 tbsps soy sauce
1 tbsp very dry sherry
1 bunch garden cress or watercress

1. Peel only the lower third of the asparagus and trim the ends of the stalks. Wash briefly and chop into 1½-inch pieces. Wash the snow peas and snip off the ends.
2. Blanch the asparagus in boiling salted water for 3 minutes. Cool in ice-cold water and drain. Do the same with the snow peas, but blanch for only 1 minute.
3. Heat the oil in a wok or large skillet. Fry the sesame seeds until golden, stirring constantly.
4. Add the asparagus and the snow peas. Cook for 5 minutes over a low heat, stirring constantly. Drizzle with the soy sauce and sherry.
5. Rinse the cress under running water. Using kitchen scissors, snip the leaves over the vegetables and stir in. Serve as an accompaniment to fillet of veal or broiled salmon. Can also be served as a vegetarian main course for two, with brown rice or new potatoes.

KOHLRABI IN GORGONZOLA SAUCE

SERVES 4
Preparation and cooking time: 25 minutes
Kcal per portion: 520
P = 23g, F = 44g, C = 8g

6 kohlrabi
salt and pepper
butter for the dish
1 cup light cream
10 ounces Gorgonzola cheese
freshly grated nutmeg
lemon juice
1 bunch chervil

1. Peel the kohlrabi and halve it. Slice it thinly, preferably in a food processor or using a mandolin. Put the slices in a saucepan with boiling salted water and cook for 3 minutes. Remove with a slotted spoon and drain well.
2. Heat the oven to 425°F.
3. Butter a large ovenproof dish and arrange the kohlrabi slices so that they overlap.
4. Bring the cream to the boil in a small saucepan. Add the Gorgonzola and melt, stirring constantly. Season with salt, pepper, nutmeg, and lemon juice.
5. Rinse the chervil and pat dry. Pull the leaves from the stalks and sprinkle most of them over the kohlrabi slices. Pour the sauce over the dish and brown in the center of the oven for 10 minutes.
6. Before serving, sprinkle with the reserved chervil leaves.
Serve with medallions of veal or poached egg. Can also be served as a vegetarian main course for two, with potatoes or sesame rice.

SWEET-AND-SOUR CARROTS

SERVES 4
Preparation and cooking time: 30 minutes
Kcal per portion: 150
P = 2g, F = 10g, C = 14g

1½ pounds carrots
salt and pepper
3 tbsps butter
3 tbsps maple syrup
juice of 1 lemon
pinch of cumin
1 bunch garden cress

1. Peel the carrots and cut diagonally into ½-inch thick slices. Put into a saucepan, just cover with

> **TIP**
>
> *Half of the carrots can be replaced by zucchini. Use fresh mint instead of garden cress for an unusual flavor.*

water, add salt, and bring to the boil. Cook for 8 minutes over a low heat.
2. Tip the carrots into a sieve and drain well.
3. Heat the butter in a large skillet. Add the maple syrup and bring to the boil. Add the carrots and sweat for 5 minutes. Sprinkle with the lemon juice. Season with salt, pepper, and cumin.
4. Rinse the garden cress under running water. Snip the leaves directly into the frying-pan.
An accompaniment to cold roast beef or roast chicken. Can also be served as a starter on a bed of fresh spinach, sprinkled with toasted sesame seeds.

MIXED PEPPERS WITH SAUSAGE

SERVES 4

Preparation and cooking time: 25 minutes
Kcal per portion: 805
P = 32g, F = 55g, C = 44g

1 large onion
2 tbsps olive oil
1½ pounds mixed red, green, and yellow peppers
½ cup tomato juice
salt and pepper
1 tsp paprika
generous pinch of cayenne
8 ounces Polish or pepperoni sausage
l bunch flat-leaved parsley

1. Slice the onion into thin rings. Heat the olive oil in a large skillet and sweat the onion rings until transparent.
2. Halve, core, de-seed, and wash the peppers. Slice across into narrow strips and add to the skillet. Pour in the tomato juice. Season with salt, pepper, paprika, and cayenne. Cook gently for 15 minutes.
3. Skin the sausage and slice, not too thickly. Combine with the vegetables and cook for 5 minutes.
4. Rinse, pat dry, and roughly chop the parsley. Just before serving, mix with the other ingredients.
Instead of spicy sausage, you could use cooked ham, sliced into strips.
Accompaniment: mashed potato.
Recommended drink: light red wine.

Halve the peppers lengthwise. Remove the core and seeds, then wash.

Thinly slice the pepper halves.

Pour the tomato juice over the strips of pepper, season, and cook for 15 minutes.

Peel and slice the sausage. Add to the vegetables and heat for a further 5 minutes.

ZUCCHINI WITH TURKEY STRIPS

SERVES 2

Preparation and cooking time: 30 minutes
Kcal per portion: 420
P = 55g, F = 18g, C = 9g

14 ounces turkey breast
2 tbsps butter
salt and white pepper
freshly grated nutmeg
4 zucchini
3 garlic cloves
1 cup vegetable broth
1 bunch flat-leaved parsley

1. Slice the turkey into thin strips.
2. Heat the butter in a large skillet. Fry the turkey strips over a high heat until golden-brown. Season with salt and pepper, sprinkle with nutmeg and set aside.
3. Cut the stalk ends from the zucchini. Wash and slice directly into the butter remaining in the pan. Cook gently until golden.
4. Crush the garlic and add to the zucchini slices.
5. Pour in the broth and bring to the boil. Add salt and pepper. Cover and cook gently for 5 minutes.
6. Meanwhile rinse, pat dry, and roughly chop the parsley. Add the turkey strips to the zucchini slices, with their meat juices, and reheat briefly.
7. Just before serving, stir in the parsley.
Chicken or pork can be used instead of the turkey fillets.
Accompaniment: mashed potato.
Recommended drink: dry cider.

MUSHROOM FRITTATA

SERVES 4

Preparation and cooking time: 30 minutes
Kcal per portion: 250
P = 13g, F = 20g, C = 4g

1 medium onion
3 tbsps olive oil
1½ pounds oyster or button mushrooms
2 garlic cloves
salt and pepper
1 bunch chives
5 eggs

1. Heat the oil in a medium-sized sauté pan. Finely dice the onion and sweat over a low heat until transparent.
2. Meanwhile, wipe the mushrooms and slice finely. Add to the skillet and sweat for 10 minutes over a medium heat. Crush the garlic and add to the pan; season with salt and pepper.
3. Finely chop the chives. Beat the eggs and stir the chives into them. Pour this over the mushrooms. Allow to set over a low heat, shaking the pan from time to time so that the mixture does not stick.
4. After about 7 minutes, slide the frittata on to a lid or plate. Turn and slide back into the skillet. Fry for a further 10 minutes, or until cooked.
The frittata looks attractive if cut into portions like a cake. It can also be served cold as a starter.
Accompaniment: tomato salad with green onions (scallions).
Recommended drink: light red wine.

SAVOY CABBAGE WITH SESAME SEEDS AND BEANSPROUTS

(see photo on page 21)

SERVES 4
Preparation and cooking time: 30 minutes
Kcal per portion: 180
P = 6g, F = 16g, C = 4g

1 head Savoy cabbage
2 cups mushrooms
3 tbsps grapeseed oil
2 garlic cloves
2 tbsps sesame seeds
fresh beansprouts
salt and pepper
generous pinch of cayenne
3 tbsps dry sherry
3 tbsps soy sauce

1. Remove the thick outer leaves from the cabbage. Quarter the cabbage and cut out the thick central stalk. Cut the quarters crossways into ¼-inch strips. Wash and drain.
2. Wipe and trim the mushrooms. Using an egg slicer, slice finely.
3. Heat the oil in a wok or large sauté pan. Fry the mushrooms briefly. Crush the garlic and add to the pan. Add the strips of cabbage and sprinkle with the sesame seeds.
4. Briefly rinse the beansprouts and add to the cabbage.
5. Season the vegetables with salt, pepper, and cayenne. Pour in the sherry and soy sauce. Cover and cook for 10 minutes over a medium heat.
This dish can be enhanced by browning some ground meat with the mushrooms – allow ½ cup per person.
Accompaniment: rice.
Recommended drink: dry sherry.

SPINACH WITH FETA AND PINENUTS

SERVES 4
Preparation and cooking time: 30 minutes
Kcal per portion: 445
P = 14g, F = 41g, C = 6g

5 cups spinach, fresh or frozen
1 small onion
2 tbsps olive oil
3 garlic cloves
4 tbsps pinenuts (pignolas)
salt and pepper
1 tsp oregano
10 ounces feta cheese

1. Wash fresh spinach and snip off the stalks. Remove frozen spinach from its packaging.
2. Chop the onion finely. Heat the oil in a large saucepan, add the onion and sweat until transparent.
3. Crush the garlic cloves and add to the onion. Add the spinach and sweat for 10 minutes.
4. Sprinkle with the pinenuts. Season with salt, pepper, and oregano.
5. Finely dice the feta or crumble it between your fingers. Sprinkle over the spinach and cook for 5 minutes over a very low heat.
Instead of pinenuts, flaked almonds can be used.
Serve as an accompaniment to broiled lamb chops.

SNOW PEAS WITH LEMON SAUCE

SERVES 4
Preparation and cooking time: 20 minutes
Kcal per portion: 325
P = 9g, F = 24g, C = 17g

5 cups snow peas
salt and white pepper
1 small onion
1 tbsp butter
1 tbsp very dry sherry
1 cup sour cream
juice of ½ lemon
2 spring onions (optional)

1. Wash the snow peas and snip off the ends. Blanch in boiling salted water for 1 minute. Cool in ice-cold water and drain well.
2. Finely chop the onion. Heat the butter in a large saucepan and sweat the

> **TIP**
>
> *If serving this dish as an appetizer the snow peas can be combined with 1 cup shrimp. Then it makes enough to serve 8.*

onion until transparent. Pour in the sherry and heat until reduced almost completely.
3. Add the sour cream and lemon juice. Cook gently for 3 minutes, then season with salt and pepper.
4. Add the snow peas to the sauce and heat for 5 minutes.
5. Optional: chop two green onions (scallions) into rings and stir into the dish.
Accompaniment: buttered rice.
Recommended drink: white or rosé wine.

SPRING CABBAGE IN SHERRY CREAM SAUCE

SERVES 4
Preparation and cooking time: 25 minutes
Kcal per portion: 410
P = 5g, F = 35g, C = 8g

1 small spring cabbage or 2 pounds collard greens
4 green onions (scallions)
1 tbsp butter
5 tbsps very dry sherry
1 cup heavy cream
1 tbsp Worcestershire sauce
salt and white pepper
2 tbsps sunflower seeds

1. Trim and quarter the cabbage, removing the thick central stalk. Cut the quarters crosswise into very fine strips. Wash and drain thoroughly.
2. Trim and wash the green onions. Chop into fine rings.
3. Heat the butter in a large saucepan and sweat the onions. Add the spring cabbage and fry, stirring, for 5 minutes.
4. Pour in the sherry, then stir in the cream. Season with Worcestershire sauce, salt, and pepper. Cover and simmer over a medium heat for 10 minutes.
5. Meanwhile dry-fry the sunflower seeds in a non-stick skillet until golden. Taste the vegetables and season again if necessary. Sprinkle with the sunflower seeds.
The sherry can be replaced by white wine or sparkling wine. Pumpkin seeds (pepitas) can be used instead of sunflower seeds.
An accompaniment to fillet of veal or steamed shellfish, such as shrimp.

Microwave Recipes

*Q*uick preparation and short but gentle cooking – that's the beauty of a microwave oven, whether you are cooking Celery in White Wine, Asparagus with Snow Peas, or hearty Hungarian Potato Goulash. There is simply no better way of cooking tender vegetables. The delicious flavors of the dishes contained in this chapter are an integral part of the microwave cooking program. For best results, remember that vegetable dishes prepared in the microwave oven have to be stirred once during cooking, that it is better to use several small containers than one large one, and that round rather than rectangular cooking dishes are best.

Okra with Tomatoes
(see recipe on page 100)

MULTICOLORED
VEGETABLE STEW

MULTICOLORED VEGETABLE STEW

SERVES 4 ■■

Microwave only
Preparation and cooking
time: 1 hour
Kcal per portion: 425
P = 5g, F = 32g, C = 23g

1 small eggplant
salt and pepper
2 small zucchini
1 red bell pepper
1 yellow bell pepper
4 floury potatoes
2 onions
2 garlic cloves
1½ cups canned tomatoes
1 sprig thyme
1 sprig rosemary
½ cup olive oil
½ cup dry red wine

Sprinkle the eggplant slices with salt and leave for 30 minutes.

1. Remove the stalk end from the eggplant. Wash the eggplant and cut it into ¼-inch slices. Sprinkle with salt and leave for about 30 minutes.
2. Meanwhile wash the zucchini and peppers. Remove the stalk ends from the zucc-

Slice the zucchini and chop the peppers into strips.

> ### TIP
> *This dish can be made with different combinations of vegetables, depending on the time of year.*

hini. Peel and wash the potatoes. Slice both vegetables. Halve, core, and de-seed the peppers; slice into fine strips. Finely chop the onions and garlic.
3. Squeeze out the eggplant slices. Arrange in alternating layers with the other vegetables in a large microwave dish. Chop the tomatoes and pour them over the other vegetables with the juice. Add the herbs, salt, and pepper. Add the oil and wine.

Season the mixed vegetables. Place in a microwave dish and pour over them the oil and wine.

Cover and cook for 26–30 minutes at 600 watts. Uncover for the last 10 minutes.
4. Leave the vegetables to stand for a short time. Mix carefully and remove the herb sprigs before serving. Serve with broiled meats or fish.

ORIENTAL-STYLE STUFFED PEPPERS

SERVES 4 ■■

Microwave only
Preparation and cooking
time: 1 hour
Kcal per portion: 680
P = 7g, F = 47g, C = 46g

8 bell peppers
2 onions
8 tbsps olive oil
uncooked long-grain rice
salt and pepper
2 tbsps currants
8–10 fresh mint leaves
½ bunch parsley
toasted pinenuts
1 tsp ground cinnamon
generous pinch ground cloves
grated rind of ½ lemon
2¼ cups canned tomato sauce
2 tbsps dry white wine

1. Wash the peppers. Cut a lid from the stalk ends and carefully remove the seeds and cores. Brush a microwave baking dish with 1 tbsp oil. Place the peppers in the dish.
2. Dice the onions and add with 3 tablespoons of oil to a microwave dish. Cook for 3–4 minutes at 600 watts. Then stir in the rice, add salt, and brown for 2 minutes at 600 watts.
3. Put the currants in the microwave with 4 tbsps water. Cover and cook for 2 minutes at 600 watts. Leave to stand for a few minutes longer.
4. Finely chop the mint and parsley. Add to the rice, together with the pinenuts and drained currants. Season with the cinnamon and cloves.
5. Stuff the peppers with the rice mixture. Do not fill more than two-thirds full as the rice will swell. Replace the lids cut from the peppers. Mix the tomato sauce with 5 tbsps oil and the wine. Pour into the dish.

Mix the pinenuts, currants, herbs, and spices with the lightly-cooked rice.

Only stuff the peppers two-thirds full with the rice mixture as the rice will swell.

6. Cover and cook for 10 minutes at 600 watts, and then for 20 minutes at 180 watts. During this time, turn the dish once through 180 degrees.

In Turkey, stuffed peppers are also served cold as a meze (appetizer).

Cooking in the microwave does not really save time in this recipe, but it helps preserve the strong individual flavors.

Recommended drink:
light, dry white wine.

HUNGARIAN POTATO GOULASH

SERVES 4 ■

Microwave only
Preparation and cooking
time: 40 minutes
Kcal per portion: 295
P = 5g, F = 20g, C = 23g

1¼ pounds waxy potatoes
2 red peppers
2 large onions
2 slices rindless Canadian
   bacon
2 tbsps oil
salt and pepper
1 tbsps paprika
1 tsp caraway seeds
2 sprigs marjoram
1 cup strong beef broth
3 tbsps sour cream
½ bunch parsley

1. Peel, wash, and finely dice the potatoes. Wash and halve the peppers; remove cores and seeds. Dice into ½-inch squares. Finely chop the onions.
2. Finely dice the bacon. Place in a microwave dish with the oil. Brown for 3–4 minutes at 600 watts.
3. Add the diced vegetables. Season with salt, pepper, paprika, caraway, and the marjoram leaves. Add the broth. Cover and cook for 17–20 minutes at 600 watts, stirring from time to time.
4. Stir the cream into the vegetables and cook, uncovered, for 4–5 minutes at 600 watts, or until thickened.
5. Chop the parsley and sprinkle it over the dish. Leave to stand for a few minutes before serving. For a spicier flavor, add finely chopped chilies.
Serve as an accompaniment to sausages or steak.

CREAMY POTATOES

SERVES 4 ■

Microwave only
Preparation and cooking
time: 30 minutes
Kcal per portion: 485
P = 6g, F= 38g, C = 29g

1½ pounds floury potatoes
1 onion
1 garlic clove
2 tbsps butter
salt and white pepper
freshly grated nutmeg
1¾ cups light cream
a few chervil leaves

1. Peel and wash the potatoes. Chop into ½-inch cubes. Finely dice the garlic. Put both into a microwave dish with the butter. Fry for 2-3 minutes at 600 watts, or until transparent.
2. Add the diced potato and season with salt, pepper, and

> **TIP**
>
> *The potato pieces should be about the same size so that they cook evenly. Do not forget to reset the microwave after stirring.*

nutmeg. Pour in the cream. Cover and cook for 15–18 minutes at 600 watts. After 5 minutes, uncover, stir once, and finish cooking uncovered.
3. Sprinkle the chervil leaves over the dish. Leave to stand for a few minutes longer.
Serve with hamburgers or steak.

BAVARIAN CABBAGE

SERVES 4 ■

Microwave only
Preparation and cooking
time: 40 minutes
Kcal per portion: 180
P = 3g, F = 16g, C = 6g

½ head white cabbage
2 slices rindless smoked
   Canadian bacon
2 tbsps oil
1 tsp sugar
1 tsp caraway seeds
1 cup ham broth
1 tbsp white wine vinegar
salt and pepper

1. Cut the stalk from the white cabbage. Remove any limp outer leaves. Wash the cabbage and slice into thin strips.
2. Finely dice the bacon. Put in a large microwave dish with oil and sugar. Glaze for 4–5 minutes at 600 watts, stirring once.
3. Add the white cabbage, stir well, and sprinkle with caraway seeds. The cabbage should not be piled too high. Add the broth and vinegar. Cover and cook for 15–18 minutes at 600 watts. Uncover, stir, and finish cooking uncovered. Leave to stand for a few more minutes before serving. Season with salt and pepper if needed. After about 10 minutes of the cooking time, thicken, if desired, with a little flour and water.
Serve with broiled sausages or roast pheasant.

KOHLRABI WITH GARDEN PEAS

SERVES 4 ■

Microwave only
Preparation and cooking
time: 30 minutes
Kcal per portion: 140
P = 4g, F = 9g, C = 8g

3 young kohlrabi with leaves
1 small onion
3 tbsps butter
5 tbsps dry white wine
salt and white pepper
1 cup fresh shelled peas
1 tbsp chopped parsley

1. Remove the leaves from the kohlrabi. Reserve the tender inner leaves. Peel the bulbs, cut into thin slices, and then into strips.
2. Chop the onion and put into a microwave dish with 2 teaspoons butter. Fry,

> **TIP**
>
> *Frozen peas can be used instead of fresh ones, and sour cream or yogurt in place of butter.*

uncovered, for 2 minutes at 600 watts. Add the strips of kohlrabi and the wine. Season with salt and pepper. Cover and cook for 6–8 minutes at 600 watts, stirring once.
3. Add the peas, cover, and cook for a further 3–4 minutes at 600 watts.
4. Carefully cut the kohlrabi leaves into thin strips. Stir them into the vegetables with the remaining butter and the parsley.
Serve as an accompaniment to roast meats.

EXOTIC LENTILS

SERVES 4 ■
Microwave only
Preparation and cooking
time: 30 minutes
Soaking time: a few hours
Kcal per portion: 300
P = 8g, F = 19g, C = 20g

⅔ cup green lentils
1 large carrot
2 celery stalks
1 onion
1–2 garlic cloves
4 tbsps oil
½ cup dry white wine
salt and pepper
2 sprigs thyme
1 bayleaf
2 tbsps sour cream or yogurt
1 tbsp chopped parsley

Place the finely chopped vegetables and the oil in a microwave dish.

Mix the soaked, drained lentils with the browned vegetables and pour in the white wine.

After half of the cooking time, stir in the sour cream or yogurt.

1. Cover the lentils with plenty of cold water and soak for 4 hours.
2. Trim and wash the carrot and celery; dice very finely. Chop the onion and the garlic finely. Put them all into a large microwave dish with the oil. Brown for 5 minutes at 600 watts, stirring once.
3. Drain the lentils and add to the dish. Add the white wine and season with salt and pepper. Add the thyme and bayleaf. Cover and cook for 6–8 minutes at 600 watts, stirring from time to time.
4. Uncover and stir the sour cream into the vegetables. Reduce, uncovered, for a further 4–5 minutes at 600 watts.
5. Remove the herbs and leave the vegetables to stand for a few minutes longer. Serve sprinkled with parsley. To make the dish creamier, blend some of the lentils in a liquidizer.
Serve as an accompaniment to boiling sausage or hamburger.

OKRA WITH TOMATOES

(see photo on page 95)

SERVES 4 ■ ■
Microwave only
Preparation and cooking
time: 45 minutes
Kcal per portion: 280
P = 9g, F = 24g, C = 32g

14 ounces okra
2 tbsps white wine vinegar
salt and pepper
1 onion
1 garlic clove
6 tbsps olive oil
6 beefsteak tomatoes
2 sprigs thyme
½ cup white wine
2 tbsps chopped parsley

Carefully remove the tops of the okra with a sharp knife.

Put the okra on a shallow dish, and sprinkle with vinegar and with salt. Leave to marinate for 30 minutes.

Stir the okra into the tomato sauce.

1. Wash the okra. Carefully remove the ends, using a sharp knife. Take care not to damage the flesh. Arrange side-by-side on a rectangular plate. Drizzle with vinegar and sprinkle with salt. Leave for at least 30 minutes.
2. Meanwhile finely chop the onion and garlic. Put them with the oil in a microwave dish. Fry for 2 minutes at 600 watts, or until transparent.
3. Wash the tomatoes. Cut a cross in the top and put them, still dripping wet, in a microwave dish. Microwave for 2–3 minutes at 600 watts. Rinse in cold water. Then peel, seed, chop, and add them to the onion. Add the thyme, salt, and pepper. Pour in the white wine. Cook gently, uncovered, for 6–8 minutes at 600 watts.
4. Mix the okra with the tomato sauce, cover and cook for 6–8 minutes at 600 watts, stirring once gently. Leave to stand for a few minutes longer. Serve sprinkled with parsley.
Serve as an accompaniment to roast chicken or broiled fish.

ONIONS STUFFED WITH VEAL

SERVES 2 ■ ■
Microwave only
Preparation and cooking time: 50 minutes
Kcal per portion: 595
P = 28g, F = 37g, C = 32g

2 Spanish onions
½ cup ground veal
2 tbsps uncooked rice
1 tbsp chopped parsley
2 tbsps tomato paste
salt and pepper
1 tsp paprika
½ cup sour cream or yogurt
2 tbsps oil
5 tbsps dry white wine

1. Peel the onions. Place in a microwave dish with 1 cup water. Cover and cook for 4–5 minutes at 600 watts, turning once.
2. Combine the veal, rice, parsley, and 1 tablespoon of tomato paste. Season with salt, pepper, and ¼ tsp paprika.
3. Cut a lid from the onions. Hollow out the inner flesh with a teaspoon. Leave at least two layers around the outside. Finely chop the onion flesh and mix half of it with the meat mixture. Stuff the onions with the mixture and put in a microwave dish.
4. Combine the sour cream or yogurt, oil, wine, remaining tomato paste, and paprika. Pour a little of the mixture over each onion. Distribute the rest, with the remaining onion, around the stuffed onions.
5. Cover and cook for 20–25 minutes at 600 watts.
Recommended drink: lager.

BEETS WITH HORSERADISH

SERVES 4 ■
Microwave only
Preparation and cooking time: 35 minutes
Kcal per portion: 130
P = 2g, F = 8g, C = 12g

1½ pounds raw beets
1 onion
3 tbsps butter
salt and pepper
2 tbsps freshly grated horseradish
1 tbsp red wine vinegar
1 tbsp maple syrup

1. Wash, peel, and coarsely grate the beetroot. Dice the onion finely and put with the butter in a microwave dish. Fry, uncovered, for 2 min-

Peel the beets and grate coarsely in a food processor.

utes at 600 watts, or until transparent.
2. Add the beets, salt, and pepper. Cover and cook for 8 minutes at 600 watts.
3. Stir the horseradish, vinegar, and syrup into the vegetables. Cook, uncovered, for a further 4–6 minutes at 600 watts.
Serve as an accompaniment to boiled beef.

LEEK AND BACON

SERVES 4 ■
Microwave only
Preparation and cooking time: 25 minutes
Kcal per portion: 275
P = 4g, F = 27g, C = 4g

2 large leeks
3 slices rindless smoked Canadian bacon
1 tbsp oil
salt and white pepper
generous pinch of soup powder
freshly grated nutmeg
⅔ cup light cream
1 tbsp lemon juice

1. Remove the roots from the leeks. Cut off almost all the green parts. Halve the leeks lengthwise, wash thoroughly and cut into ¼-inch slices.
2. Finely dice the bacon. Put the bacon and the oil into a large microwave dish. Fry, uncovered, for 3–4 minutes at 600 watts, until the fat is transparent.
3. Add the leeks. They should not be piled too high. Season with salt, pepper, soup powder, and nutmeg; add the cream. Cover and cook for 8–10 minutes at 600 watts. After 5 minutes, uncover, stir, and continue cooking uncovered. Season with the lemon juice.
Serve as an accompaniment to sausages or boiled beef.

MIXED PEPPERS

SERVES 4 ■
Microwave only
Preparation and cooking time: 40 minutes
Kcal per portion: 225
P = 3g, F = 19g, C = 10g

2 small red peppers
2 small yellow peppers
2 small green peppers
1 Bermuda onion
1 garlic clove
2 large beefsteak tomatoes
5 tbsps olive oil
2 sprigs thyme
1 bayleaf
salt and pepper
1 tbsp minced parsley

1. Halve, core, and de-seed the peppers. Slice the flesh into thin strips. Finely dice the garlic.

> **TIP**
>
> *This dish can be enhanced by adding green or black olives.*

2. Cut a cross in the top of the tomatoes. Wash them and place in a microwave dish dripping wet. Microwave for 3–4 minutes at 600 watts. Cool in cold water, peel, and halve. Remove the stalk ends and seeds.
3. Place all the chopped vegetables in a large microwave dish. Do not pile too high. Pour the oil over them. Add the herbs and season with salt and pepper. Cover and cook for 18–20 minutes at 600 watts, stirring from time to time.
4. Remove the herbs and sprinkle with parsley.
Serve as an accompaniment to boiled beef or steak.

ASPARAGUS WITH SNOW PEAS

SERVES 4 ■
Microwave only
Preparation and cooking
time: 40 minutes
Kcal per portion: 95
P = 5g, F = 7g, C = 7g

white asparagus
½ cup water
pinch of sugar
salt
2 tbsps butter
1 cup snow peas
a few sprigs of chervil
a little grated orange rind

1. Peel the asparagus stalks. Cut off the ends and chop into 2-inch pieces. Reserve the tips. Place the rest in a

> **TIP**
>
> *The thickness of the asparagus spears and their quality determine how long this dish takes to cook.*

microwave dish. Add the water. Add salt, sprinkle with sugar, and add 1 tsp butter. Cover, and cook for 5–6 minutes at 600 watts.
2. Meanwhile, snip the ends off the snow peas and wash them. Mix the snow peas and asparagus tips with the rest of the asparagus. Cover and cook for a further 4–5 minutes at 600 watts.
3. Pull off the chervil leaves. Mix into the vegetables, together with the orange rind and remaining butter. Leave to stand, covered, for a few minutes longer.
Serve as an accompaniment to veal or turkey, steak, or baked and broiled fish.

Carefully peel the asparagus spears, using an asparagus peeler or swivel vegetable peeler.

Mix the snow peas with the pre-cooked asparagus.

Before serving, mix orange rind, chervil leaves, and butter into the vegetables.

SALSIFY IN CARAWAY SAUCE

SERVES 2 ■
Microwave only
Preparation and cooking
time: 1 hour
Kcal per portion: 340
P = 5g, F = 32g, C = 7g

1 quart water
2 tbsps vinegar
1¼ pounds salsify
salt and white pepper
1 tbsp caraway seeds
1 cup light cream
1 tsp red wine vinegar
juice and rind of ½ lemon
1 tbsp chopped parsley

1. Put the water and vinegar into a large bowl. Wash and peel the salsify. Place in the bowl of water and vinegar so that it does not discolor.
2. Chop the salsify into even-sized pieces. Place in a microwave dish and add 1 cup water. Add salt and half the caraway seeds.
3. Cover and cook for 20–25 minutes at 600 watts. At the end of the cooking time, remove the vegetables from the oven. Leave to stand, covered, for a few more minutes.
4. During this time put the cream, the remaining caraway seeds, vinegar, lemon juice and rind, salt, and pepper in a microwave dish. Reduce by half for 8–10 minutes at 600 watts, until smooth.
5. Drain the salsify in a sieve and mix into the cream sauce. Heat, uncovered, for 3–4 minutes. Serve sprinkled with parsley.
Serve as an accompaniment to roast beef, steak, or hamburger.

CELERY IN WHITE WINE

SERVES 2 ■
Microwave only
Preparation and cooking
time: 30 minutes
Kcal per portion: 280
P = 3g, F = 21g, C = 8g

1 head celery
2 shallots
4 tbsps butter
salt and white pepper
½ cup dry white wine
½ tsp flour
1 tbsp chopped herbs (parsley, basil, tarragon, chives)

1. Trim the celery. Cut off any leaves and reserve. Separate the stalks and wash. Chop into ¾-inch pieces.
2. Dice the shallots and put in a microwave dish with 3 tsps butter. Fry for 2 minutes at 600 watts or until transparent. Then add the celery. Season with salt and pepper. Add the white wine. Cover and cook for 10 minutes at 600 watts.
3. Knead the remaining butter with the flour. Stir into the vegetables. Reduce, uncovered, for 4–5 minutes at 600 watts.
Serve sprinkled with herbs and finely-chopped celery leaves.
Serve as an accompaniment to braised meats.

GREEK-STYLE MUSHROOMS

SERVES 2 ■
Microwave only
Preparation and cooking
time: 25 minutes
Kcal per portion: 305
P = 7g, F = 23g, C = 6g

1¼ pounds mushrooms
2 small onions
1 bayleaf
1 sprig thyme
generous pinch of ground
  coriander
juice of ½ lemon
3 tbsps olive oil
½ cup dry white wine
salt and white pepper
1 tbsp chopped parsley

1. Wipe the mushrooms and slice them. Finely dice the onions. Put both in a microwave dish and add the bayleaf, thyme, and coriander. Pour in the lemon juice, oil, and wine. Season with salt and pepper.

TIP

Mushrooms cooked in this way also taste delicious as a cold appetizer. Brown store mushrooms have a stronger, more aromatic flavor than white ones.

2. Cover, and microwave for 15 minutes at 600 watts, stirring once during this time.
3. Remove the herbs. Stir the parsley into the mushrooms and serve.
Serve as an accompaniment to hamburger and steaks.

Wipe the mushrooms and cut off the stalk ends.

Place all the ingredients in a microwave dish; they will only need to cook for 15 minutes.

Take care when removing the mushrooms from the oven – the bowl will be very hot.

SWISS-STYLE CARROT PURÉE

SERVES 4 ■
Microwave only
Preparation and cooking
time: 35 minutes
Kcal per portion: 225
P = 3g, F = 16g, C = 16g

4 large floury potatoes
1¼ pounds carrots
⅔ cup light cream
salt
pinch of sugar
2 tbsps butter
2 tbsps finely chopped chervil

1. Peel, wash, and finely chop the potatoes and carrots. Put in a microwave dish with the cream. Add the salt and sugar. Cover and cook for 15–18 minutes at 600 watts, stirring from time to time.

TIP

If you can get young, bunched carrots in the spring, make sure they have fresh, juicy leaves. Remove the leaves immediately since they draw the juice out of the carrots.

2. Blend the potato and carrot mixture in a liquidizer. Stir in the butter in small knobs. Put the carrot purée into a bowl and sprinkle with chervil.
Serve as an accompaniment to braised meats or hamburger.

ZUCCHINI WITH TOMATO

SERVES 2 ■
Microwave only
Preparation and cooking
time: 30 minutes
Kcal per portion: 265
P = 6g, F = 23g, C = 8g

2 zucchini
½ cup button mushrooms
2 beefsteak tomatoes
2 shallots
1 tbsp oil
3 tsps butter
1 sprig thyme
salt and pepper
½ tsp paprika
2 tbsps sour cream or plain
  yogurt
2 tbsps chopped parsley

1. Wash the zucchini and cut off the ends. Wipe the mushrooms. Slice both vegetables finely.
2. Cut a cross in the top of the tomatoes. Place dripping wet in a microwave dish, cover and microwave for 2–3 minutes at 600 watts. Then rinse in cold water, peel, and dice finely, discarding the stalk ends and seeds.
3. Finely chop the shallots and put with the oil and butter in a microwave dish. Fry for 2 minutes at 600 watts, or until transparent.
4. Add the sliced zucchini and mushrooms. Sprinkle with individual thyme leaves. Season with salt, pepper, and paprika. Stir in the sour cream or yogurt, cover, and cook for 4 minutes at 600 watts.
5. Add the diced tomato. Stir and cook, uncovered, for a further 4–5 minutes at 600 watts.
6. Sprinkle with parsley and leave to stand for a little while longer before serving. Serve as an accompaniment to hamburgers or steaks.

Lean Cuisine

As far as vegetables are concerned, lean cuisine has an added advantage. Eating light healthy food does not mean having to do without your favorite dishes. In many cases, a dish designed as an accompaniment can even be transformed into an entrée. Simply increase the amount of vegetables, herbs, and other ingredients, to produce a balanced low-calorie meal. This applies just as much to Asparagus Ragoût with Broccoli or Tomato and Potato Stew as it does to appetizing Mixed Vegetables in Coconut Milk.

Fennel and Pears
(see recipe on page 122)

LEEK AND CARROT MEDLEY

SERVES 4 ■

Preparation and cooking time: 40 minutes
Kcal per portion: 135
P = 2g, F = 12g, C = 6g

3 medium leeks
3 medium carrots
3 tbsps olive oil
salt and white pepper
½ cup strong chicken broth
juice of ½ lemon
1 tbsp chopped parsley

1. Remove the roots from the leeks. Halve them lengthwise, wash thoroughly under

> **TIP**
>
> ***This also tastes delicious cold. Yogurt flavored with garlic can be served with it, if desired.***

running water, and cut into ½-inch pieces. Scrub or scrape the carrots. Slice first lengthwise, then cut into narrow strips about 2 inches long.
2. Heat the oil in a large flameproof casserole. Fry the leeks over a medium heat until golden. Season with salt and pepper and add the broth. Cover and simmer for about 10 minutes over a low heat.
3. Stir in the carrot and cook for about 15–20 minutes.
4. Season the vegetables with lemon juice and, if necessary, more salt and pepper. Sprinkle with parsley.
Serve as an accompaniment to any meat dish.

CARROTS WITH SHERRY

SERVES 2 ■

Preparation and cooking time: 30 minutes
Kcal per portion: 220
P = 3g, F = 15g, C = 9g

1 bunch young carrots with leaves
1 shallot
3 tsps butter
salt and white pepper
3 tbsps dry sherry
3 tsps pinenuts

1. Remove the leaves from the carrots, reserving a few small ones. Scrub and finely slice the carrots. Finely dice the shallot.
2. Heat the butter in a small flameproof casserole. Sweat the shallot over a medium heat until transparent. Add the sliced carrot and brown lightly, stirring constantly. Add salt, then pour in the sherry. Cover and cook over a medium heat. The vegetables should still be firm.
3. Meanwhile dry-fry the pinenuts in a small skillet. Finely chop the carrot leaves.
4. Season the carrots with pepper. Sprinkle with carrot leaves and pine nuts.
Serve as an accompaniment to roast chicken or braised veal.

SHALLOTS AND PEAS

SERVES 2 ■

Preparation and cooking time: 45 minutes
Kcal per portion: 195
P = 8g, F = 9g, C = 21g

10 shallots
3 tsps butter
½ tsp sugar
6 tbsps strong chicken broth
1 cup fresh shelled peas
salt and white pepper
1 tbsp chopped parsley

1. Heat the butter in a flameproof casserole. Quarter the shallots, put in the pan, and sprinkle with sugar. Glaze, stirring constantly, over a low heat until golden-brown. Add the broth, cover, and simmer for about 10 minutes.
2. When the shallots have become syrupy and are almost cooked, add the peas. Season with salt and pepper. Cook for about 5 minutes over a low heat. Serve sprinkled with parsley. Frozen peas can be used instead of fresh peas.
Serve as an accompaniment to meat stews or braised chicken.

GREEN BEANS WITH BLACK OLIVES

SERVES 4 ■

Preparation and cooking time: 40 minutes
Kcal per portion: 215
P = 5g, F = 12g, C = 16g

1½ pounds young green beans
4 small shallots
2 tbsps olive oil
2 thyme sprigs
salt and pepper
½ cup dry white wine
2 tbsps pitted black olives
2 tbsps chopped parsley

1. Trim the beans and wash them. Leave small beans

> **TIP**
>
> ***The cooking time depends on the size and tenderness of the beans. Always test their crispness during cooking.***

whole, snap larger ones in half. Chop or quarter the shallots.
2. Heat the olive oil in a flameproof casserole and brown the shallots. Add the beans and thyme sprigs. Season with salt and pepper and pour in the white wine. Cover and simmer over a medium heat. After about 5 minutes, stir in the olives, then cook until the beans are done but still firm.
3. Discard the thyme and sprinkle with parsley.
Serve as an accompaniment to roast lamb.

ASPARAGUS RAGOÛT
WITH BROCCOLI

ASPARAGUS RAGOÛT WITH BROCCOLI

SERVES 4 ■
*Preparation and cooking
time: 50 minutes
Kcal per portion: 195
P = 5g, F = 18g, C = 5g*

1½ pounds white asparagus
8 ounces broccoli
salt and white pepper
pinch of sugar
2 tbsps butter
⅔ cup light cream
1 tsp flour
pinch of cayenne pepper
a little grated lemon rind
lemon juice to taste
1 egg yolk
1 tbsp finely-chopped chives

Peel the asparagus and divide the broccoli into flowerets.

1. Carefully peel the asparagus spears. If necessary, cut off the ends, then chop.

> **TIP**
>
> *A light meal can be produced by mixing cooked peeled shrimp with the vegetables.*

Thicken the asparagus sauce with beaten egg yolk.

Wash the broccoli and divide into small flowerets. Finely chop the stalks.
2. Bring a generous amount of water to the boil, containing salt, sugar and 2 tsps butter. Boil the asparagus for about 10–15 minutes, depending on the thickness of the spears, so that they are still firm. Cook the broccoli flowerets and stalk pieces in boiling salted water. They should still be firm.
3. Drain the asparagus spears and reserve the water. Measure out 2 cups of the asparagus cooking water. Mix with the cream and cook over medium heat until reduced by half.
4. Knead the remaining but-

Mix the cooked vegetables into the sauce.

ter with the flour. Using a whisk, beat this into the boiling asparagus broth to thicken it. Cook for a few minutes over a high heat. Season with salt, pepper, cayenne, grated lemon rind and lemon juice.
5. Add the asparagus and the well-drained broccoli to the sauce. Whisk the egg yolk with a little sauce and use to thicken the ragoût. If necessary, season again, then sprinkle with chives.
Serve as an accompaniment to pork chops.

ENDIVE IN ORANGE BUTTER

SERVES 4 ■
*Preparation and cooking
time: 30 minutes
Kcal per portion: 85
P = 2g, F = 6g, C = 5g*

4 heads endive
2 tbsps butter
1 tsp sugar
juice and grated rind of 1
   orange
salt
cayenne pepper
a few mint leaves
orange segments to garnish
   (optional)

1. Remove any limp outer leaves from the endive and cut the heads in half. Remove the bitter cores.

> **TIP**
>
> *Endive is an extremely low-calorie vegetable, although rich in minerals. Its slightly bitter taste is pleasantly reduced by the addition of orange juice.*

2. Heat the butter in a flameproof casserole. Add the sugar, orange rind, and orange juice. Season with a pinch of salt and cayenne. Heat through quickly.
3. Toss the endive halves in the orange butter. Cover and cook, cut surfaces downward, for about 10 minutes. Baste with the braising juices from time to time.
4. Serve garnished with orange segments if desired. Serve as an accompaniment to veal or turkey steaks.

Remove the limp leaves from the endive.

Carefully cut the bitter core from the endive halves.

Toss the endive halves in the orange butter.

CUCUMBER WITH FISH STUFFING

SERVES 2 ■■
Preparation and cooking time: 45 minutes
Kcal per portion: 200
P = 23g, F = 4g, C = 4g

1 medium cucumber
salt and white pepper
8 ounces white fish fillets
1 egg white
1 tbsp sour cream
2 tbsps finely chopped dill
pinch of cayenne pepper
juice of ½ lemon
½ cup strong fish broth

1. Partially peel the cucumber, leaving green stripes. Cut into four pieces, about 2½ inches long. Hollow them out and sprinkle inside and

> **TIP**
>
> *If you wish to serve a sauce with the cucumber, thicken the fish broth with plain yogurt.*

outside with salt. Finely dice the remaining cucumber.
2. For the fish stuffing, cut the fish into pieces and blend well in a liquidizer. Thoroughly mix in the egg white, san cream and 1 tablespoon dill. Season with salt, pepper, cayenne, and lemon juice.
3. Stuff the cucumber pieces with the mixture. Place in a steamer and arrange the diced cucumber around them.
4. Pour the fish broth into the bottom half of the steamer. Place the steamer over the broth. Cover and steam for about 10 minutes. Serve sprinkled with dill.

TOMATO AND POTATO STEW

SERVES 4 ■
Preparation and cooking time: 50 minutes
Kcal per portion: 255
P = 8g, F = 12g, C = 30g

1 onion
1-2 garlic cloves
4 beefsteak tomatoes
2 tbsps olive oil
1 sprig thyme
1 sprig rosemary
salt and pepper
1¼ pounds floury potatoes
8 tbsps chicken broth
1 tbsp minced parsley
1 tbsp chopped basil

1. Finely dice the onion and garlic. Blanch, peel, core, and chop the tomatoes.
2. Heat the oil in a flameproof casserole and lightly brown the onion and garlic. Add the tomatoes, thyme, and rosemary. Season with salt and pepper. Cover and cook over a low heat for about 5 minutes.
3. Meanwhile wash and finely dice the potatoes. Stir into the tomato mixture and pour the broth over them. Cover and cook over a low heat for about 30 minutes, stirring from time to time. Season again, and serve sprinkled with parsley and basil.
Serve as an accompaniment to hamburger or fried meats.

SPICY MIXED PEPPERS

SERVES 4 ■
Preparation and cooking time: 40 minutes
Kcal per portion: 185
P = 5g, F = 9g, C = 16g

2 green peppers
2 red peppers
1 Bermuda onion
2 garlic cloves
4 anchovy fillets
2 tbsps olive oil
salt and pepper
½ tsp dried mixed herbs
½ cup dry white wine
½ cup canned sweetcorn
2 tbsps chopped parsley

1. Wash and halve the peppers; remove the cores and seeds. Chop the halves into small squares. Dice the onion and garlic; finely chop the anchovies.
2. Heat the oil in a large nonstick skillet. Lightly brown the anchovies and garlic. Gradually add the vegetables, stirring constantly, and cook over a medium heat for a few minutes. Season with salt and pepper and sprinkle with the herbs. Pour in the wine. Cover and cook over a low heat for about 15–20 minutes, stirring from time to time.
3. Stir in the sweetcorn and bring to the boil over a high heat. Stir in the parsley just before serving.
Serve as an accompaniment to hamburger.

SWEET-AND-SOUR BEETS

SERVES 2 ■
Preparation and cooking time: 50 minutes
Kcal per portion: 230
P = 2g, F = 15g, C = 14g

14 ounces raw beets
4 small shallots
2 tbsps oil
1 tsp coriander (cilantro) seeds
salt and white pepper
1 tbsp maple syrup
1 tsp red wine vinegar
5 tbsps red wine
a few coriander (cilantro) sprigs

1. Wash and peel the beetroot. Cut into ¼-inch slices, then into strips. Quarter the shallots.
2. Heat the oil in a flameproof casserole and brown the shallot quarters.

> **TIP**
>
> *Beets are also delicious served with cold creamy yogurt or sour cream. When buying beets for this dish be sure to get the raw vegetable, as beets are often sold pre-cooked.*

3. Add the beets and crushed coriander seeds. Season with salt and pepper. Pour in the maple syrup, vinegar, and red wine. Stir well, cover and cook for about 20–30 minutes.
4. Serve sprinkled with individual coriander (cilantro) leaves.
Serve as an accompaniment to stews and hamburgers.

OYSTER MUSHROOMS WITH TOMATOES

SERVES 2 ■
Preparation and cooking time: 25 minutes
Kcal per portion: 220
P = 4g, F = 16g, C = 12g

10 ounces oyster mushrooms
1 small onion
1 garlic clove
2 tbsps oil
salt and pepper
1 sprig oregano
4 tbsps dry white wine
2 beefsteak tomatoes
1 tbsp chopped parsley or basil

1. Cut the ends off the oyster mushrooms. Wipe, pat dry, and divide into pieces. Finely dice the onion and garlic.
2. Heat the oil in a nonstick skillet. Lightly brown the onion and garlic. Add the mushrooms and sweat them for a few minutes, turning them in the oil. Sprinkle with salt,

> **TIP**
>
> *Lay slices of Mozzarella over the cooked vegetables and cover for a few minutes to melt the cheese.*

pepper, and individual oregano leaves. Pour in the wine, cover, and cook over a low heat for about 10 minutes.
3. Meanwhile blanch and peel the tomatoes. Dice finely, without the stalk ends or core. Scatter over them the mushrooms and heat briefly. Serve sprinkled with herbs.

SAVOY CABBAGE ROLLS WITH WILD MUSHROOMS

SERVES 2 ■ ■
Preparation and cooking time: 45 minutes
Kcal per portion: 260
P = 16g, F = 17g, C = 8g

4 large clean Savoy cabbage leaves
salt and pepper
8 ounces wild mushrooms
1 shallot
3 tsps butter
⅔ cup cottage cheese
2 tbsps chopped mixed herbs (basil, parsley, chervil)
2 tbsps grated Cheddar cheese
½ cup chicken broth
1 tbsp sour cream

1. Blanch the cabbage leaves in plenty of boiling salted water for a few minutes. Remove from the water using a slotted spoon. Plunge briefly into ice-cold water, then drain.
2. Wipe the mushrooms and halve larger ones if necessary. Dice the shallot finely. Heat the butter in a nonstick skillet and fry the shallot until transparent. Add the mushrooms and brown lightly, stirring constantly.
3. Let the mushrooms cool slightly. Heat the oven to 400°F.
4. Mix together the cottage cheese, herbs, and Cheddar cheese. Add the mushrooms. Season generously with salt and pepper.
5. Spread out the Savoy cabbage leaves. Spread the mushroom mixture over them. Fold both sides of each leaf over the stuffing. Roll up from end to end like a burrito and put side-by-side in a baking dish. Pour broth over them, cover, and cook for about 25 minutes. Ten minutes before the end of the cooking time remove the

After cooling, stir the browned mushrooms and shallots into the herb-and-cheese mixture.

Spread the mushroom and cottage cheese mixture over the Savoy cabbage leaves. Fold the long edges inwards, then roll up.

lid, spoon the juices over the rolls, and brush with the sour cream.
Use fresh wild chanterelles for preference, but if they are unavailable, ceps (porcini) or button mushrooms can be used.
Serve as an accompaniment to game. Can also be served on its own as a starter or a vegetarian main course. In the latter case, double the quantities.

GREEN ONIONS WITH MUSHROOMS

SERVES 2 ■
Preparation and cooking time: 35 minutes
Kcal per portion: 185
P = 4g, F = 18g, C = 2g

1 bunch green onions (scallions)
2 cups button mushrooms
1 tbsp sesame oil
salt and white pepper
generous pinch of ground lemongrass
generous pinch of ground coriander
generous pinch of ground turmeric
1-2 tbsps soy sauce
a few coriander (cilantro) sprigs

1. Trim and wash the green onions (scallions). Chop into thin, diagonal slices, including some of the green parts. Wipe and finely slice the mushrooms.

> **TIP**
>
> *If you like ethnic cooking, you should grow your own coriander (cilantro). It thrives easily and adds an interesting flavor to many dishes.*

2. Heat the oil in a wok or sauté pan. Stir-fry the onions briefly.
3. Add the mushrooms, salt, and pepper. Sprinkle with the spices. Stir-fry until the vegetables are cooked but still firm. Season with the soy sauce and serve garnished with coriander (cilantro) sprigs.
Serve as an accompaniment to fried fish or turkey steaks.

GOLDEN CAULIFLOWER

SERVES 2

Preparation and cooking time: 35 minutes
Kcal per portion: 245
P = 5g, F = 20g, C = 8g

1 small cauliflower
1 onion
1 garlic clove
1 dried chili
2 tbsps oil
1 tsp curry powder
generous pinch of ground
    saffron
salt and white pepper
3 tbsps rice wine or dry
    sherry
½ cup Greek yogurt
a few chervil sprigs

1. Trim the cauliflower and divide into small flowerets. Finely dice the onion and garlic. De-seed and finely dice the chili.
2. Heat the oil in a wok or sauté panand sweat the onion and garlic until

> **TIP**
>
> *Sambal oelek is an Indonesian spice. It is obtainable from gourmet foodstores and oriental markets.*

until transparent. Add the chili, curry powder, and saffron and fry briefly.
3. Add the cauliflower flowerets and season with salt and pepper. Cook over a medium heat, stirring constantly, until golden. Add the rice wine or sherry. Cover and cook over a low heat for about 10 minutes, stirring from time to time.
4. Stir the yogurt until smooth and mix into the vegetables. Sprinkle with chervil. An accompaniment to white fish or jumbo shrimp.

MIXED VEGETABLES IN COCONUT MILK

SERVES 4

Preparation and cooking time: 45 minutes
Kcal per portion: 160
P = 5g, F = 12g, C = 8g

4 small shallots
1 garlic clove
3 celery stalks
2 small carrots
½ cup mushrooms
1 Chinese (Nappa) cabbage
½ cup snow peas
3 tbsps oil
salt and pepper
1 tsp finely grated ginger root
½ tsp ground lemongrass
generous pinch of cayenne
    pepper
generous pinch of sambal
    oelek (optional)
½ cup unsweetened coconut
    milk
1 tbsp minced parsley

1. Cut the shallots into wedges and finely chop the garlic. Trim and wash the other vegetables.
2. Slice the celery into thin slices. Slice the carrots, mushrooms, and Chinese cabbage into thin strips. Leave the snow peas whole.
3. Heat the oil in a wok or sauté pan. Brown the vegetables separately, stirring constantly. Season with salt, add the spices, and add the coconut milk. Bring to the boil and cook over a low heat for a few minutes. The vegetables should be cooked but still firm.
4. Serve sprinkled with parsley.
Serve as an accompaniment to oriental-style meat dishes.

STIR-FRIED KOHLRABI

SERVES 2

Preparation and cooking time: 30 minutes
Kcal per portion: 405
P = 8g, F = 36g, C = 12g

2 medium kohlrabi
1 small onion
2 tbsps oil
½ tsp mild curry powder
2 tbsps soy sauce
2 tbsps sunflower seeds

1. Remove any leaves from the kohlrabi and reserve them. Peel the kohlrabi, slice thinly, then cut into strips. Finely dice the onion.
2. Heat the oil in a wok or sauté pan and sweat the onion until transparent. Add the strips of kohlrabi and fry gently over a medium heat, stirring constantly. Sprinkle with curry powder, add the soy sauce and continue to stir-fry until the kohlrabi is cooked.
3. Dry-fry the sunflower seeds in a skillet.
4. Finely slice the reserved kohlrabi leaves. Sprinkle them over the vegetables, with the sunflower seeds.
Serve as an accompaniment to curried chicken breast.

FRIED CELERIAC WITH SESAME SEED CRUST

SERVES 2

Preparation and cooking time: 1 hour
Kcal per portion: 325
P = 25g, F = 21g, C = 12g

1 celeriac (celery root)
1 small egg
1 tbsp cracked wheat
2 tbsp sesame seeds
salt and white pepper
2 tbsps oil

1. Wash the celeriac; leave it whole and un-peeled. Boil for about 40 minutes or until cooked but not too soft in plenty of boiling salted water.
2. Cool the celeriac briefly in cold water, then pull off the skin or peel it.
3. Chop the celeriac into ½-in slices. Beat the egg with a fork. Combine the cracked wheat and sesame seeds.

> **TIP**
>
> *Cooking the celeriac in the pressure-cooker saves a great deal of time. Peel it while still hot, as the skin is easier to remove.*

Lightly dust the celeriac slices with salt and pepper. Turn the slices first in the egg, then in the sesame seed mixture.
4. Heat the oil in a large non-stick skillet. Fry the celeriac slices over a medium heat for about 3 minutes on each side, until golden.
Serve as an accompaniment to roast venison or medallions of venison. Can also be served as a light meal with cranberries.

ZUCCHINI PATTIES

SERVES 4

Preparation and cooking time: 30 minutes
Kcal per portion: 190
P = 6g, F = 16g, C = 2g

2 medium zucchini
1 small onion
1 garlic clove
½ bunch parsley
4 ounces feta cheese
1 egg
salt and pepper
3 tbsps oil

1. Wash the zucchini. Cut off the ends and grate the flesh coarsely.
2. Finely dice the onion and garlic. Chop the parsley and mash the cheese.
3. Mix all these ingredients together. Beat the egg. Add to the other ingredients and

---

TIP

Mix some coarsely chopped sunflower seeds into the mixture.

---

mix thoroughly. Season the mixture generously with salt and pepper.
4. Heat the oil in a large non-stick skillet. Using a tablespoon, place small balls of the mixture in the hot fat. Press flat with the back of a spoon and fry over a medium heat for about 3–4 minutes on each side. Drain on absorbent paper and serve immediately.
Serve as an accompaniment to roast lamb or veal. Can also be served as a meal for two with rémoulade sauce.

ZUCCHINI STUFFED WITH CHICKEN AND SHRIMP

SERVES 4

Preparation and cooking time: 1 hour
Kcal per portion: 230
P = 25g, F = 9g, C = 11g

4 medium zucchini
1 tbsp oil
2 tbsps chopped onion
10 ounces chicken breast
1 tbsp minced dill
1 egg
1 tbsp breadcrumbs
½ cup cooked peeled bay
    shrimp
salt and white pepper
1 tbsp curry powder
freshly grated ginger root
cayenne pepper
1 tbsp butter
½ cup strong chicken
    broth

1. Wash the zucchini. Halve lengthwise and hollow out, leaving a thin shell. Finely chop the flesh.
2. Heat the oil in a nonstick skillet. Sweat the onion with the zucchini.
3. Heat the oven to 400°F.
4. Finely grind the chicken in a food processor. Mash into a smooth meat stuffing with the zucchini mixture, dill, egg, and breadcrumbs. Stir in the shrimp. Season well with salt, pepper, curry powder, ginger, and cayenne. Stuff the mixture into the hollowed-out zucchini halves.
5. Butter a large baking dish and put in the zucchini. Dot the stuffing with butter and bake for about 30 minutes. After 15 minutes, add the chicken broth. Bake another 15 minutes or until lightly browned.

Halve the zucchini lengthwise. Hollow out and finely chop the flesh.

Mash together the processed chicken, fried vegetables, dill, egg, and breadcrumbs.

Mix the shrimp into the meat stuffing; add seasoning and spices.

Fill the hollowed-out zucchini halves with the chicken-and-shrimp mixture.

TOMATOES STUFFED WITH FETA CHEESE

SERVES 4

Preparation and cooking time: 1 hour
Kcal per portion: 145
P = 4g, F = 12g, C = 4g

8 medium ripe tomatoes
salt and pepper
1 onion
2 garlic cloves
1 thyme sprig
1 oregano sprig
2 parsley stalks
4 ounces feta cheese
1 egg
1 tbsp breadcrumbs
1-2 tbsps olive oil

1. Cut a lid from the tomatoes and reserve it. Hollow out the tomatoes using a small spoon. Season the insides with salt and pepper.
2. Heat the oven to 400°F.
3. For the stuffing, finely dice the onion and garlic. Pull the leaves from the thyme and oregano. Mince these, together with the parsley. Mash the feta with a fork or blend in a liquidizer. Add the egg and the breadcrumbs. Mix to a smooth paste with the other ingredients. If necessary, season with salt and pepper.
4. Stuff the tomatoes with the mixture and cover with the lids. Brush a small baking dish with some of the oil. Put in the tomatoes and brush with the remaining oil. Cook in the center of the oven for about 25–30 minutes.
Accompaniment:
green salad and unpeeled boiled potatoes. Can also be served cold as a starter.

FENNEL AND PEARS

(see photo on page 108)

SERVES 2 ■
*Preparation and cooking
time: 35 minutes
Kcal per portion: 260
P = 6g, f = 9g, C = 28g*

*2 small fennel bulbs
2 pears
juice of ½ lemon
2 tsps butter or margarine
salt and white pepper
cayenne pepper
½ cup dry white wine
¼ cup shelled peas*

1. Wash and trim the fennel bulbs. Cut off and reserve any green leaves. Halve and thinly slice the bulbs. Peel, halve, and core the pears.

TIP

*The pears used
for this dish
should not be
too soft.*

Slice the halves lengthwise and sprinkle with lemon juice.
2. Heat the butter or margarine in a flameproof casserole. Fry the fennel strips lightly. Season with salt, pepper, and a pinch of cayenne; pour in the wine. Cover and simmer for about 15 minutes.
3. Add the pear slices and peas. Cover and cook for just a few minutes.
4. Finely chop the reserved fennel leaves and sprinkle over the vegetables.
Serve as an accompaniment to Italian-style braised veal.

The fennel leaves can be used for garnishing.

Thinly slice the fennel bulbs and the pears.

Add the pear slices and peas to the braised strips of fennel.

CELERY WITH MOZZARELLA

SERVES 4 ■
*Preparation and cooking
time: 1 hour
Kcal per portion: 245
P = 5g, F = 9g, C = 16g*

*2 heads celery
2 tbsps butter
salt and white pepper
½ cup dry white wine
4 beefsteak tomatoes
10 pitted black olives
6–8 basil leaves
4 ounces mozzarella cheese*

1. Cut the bottom and any green leaves from the celery. Cut in half lengthwise.
2. Heat the butter in a large flameproof casserole. Turn the celery halves in the butter, season with salt and pepper, and pour in the wine. Cover and simmer gently for about 20 minutes.
3. Meanwhile blanch, peel, core, and finely dice the tomatoes. Slice the olives and cut the basil leaves into thin strips. Combine with the diced tomato. Season with salt and pepper. Cut the Mozzarella into thin slices.
4. Heat the broiler to medium.
5. Turn the celery over so that the cut surfaces face upward. Cover with the tomato mixture, then with cheese. Brown under the broiler for 10 minutes.
Serve as an accompaniment to fillet steak or rissoles. Can be served with mashed potato as a vegetarian main course for two.

SPINACH WITH YOGURT

SERVES 4 ■
*Preparation and cooking
time: 35 minutes
Kcal per portion: 90
P = 3g, F = 8g, C = 2g*

*1¼ pounds young spinach
1 onion
2-3 garlic cloves
2 tbsps oil
1 small dried chili
a little freshly grated ginger
 root
1 tsp curry powder
salt and white pepper
¾ cup Greek-style (thick,
 plain) yogurt
tomato strips to garnish*

1. Trim the spinach and remove the thicker stalks. Thoroughly wash the leaves several times and drain.
2. Finely dice the onion and one garlic clove. Heat the oil in a wok or sauté pan. Sweat the onion and garlic until transparent.
3. De-seed and finely chop the chili. Add to the pan with the grated ginger and curry powder. Lightly brown over a medium heat. Stir in the spinach leaves, cover, and leave for a few minutes until they collapse.
4. Meanwhile, crush the remaining garlic cloves and mix with the yogurt. Season generously with salt and pepper.
5. Arrange the spinach in rings on warmed plates. Pour the garlic-flavored yogurt into the center. If desired, sprinkle with a little curry powder, toasted almonds, or pistachio nuts. Garnish with thin strips of tomato.
Serve as an accompaniment to broiled kabobs.

Index